Health, Safety, and Nutrition

Ann Watts
and
Phygenia Young

DELMAR
CENGAGE Learning™

Australia • Brazil • Japan • Korea • Mexico • Singapore • Spain • United Kingdom • United States

OUACHITA TECHNICAL COLLEGE

DELMAR
CENGAGE Learning™

Health, Safety, and Nutrition
Ann Watts
Phygenia Young

For product information and technology assistance, contact us
at **Cengage Learning Customer & Sales Support, 1-800-354-9706**
For permission to use material from this text or product, submit all requests online at **www.cengage.com/permissions**
Further permissions questions can be emailed to **permissionrequest@cengage.com**

Library of Congress Catalog Card Number: 2005032317

ISBN-13: 978-1-4180-1166-6
ISBN-10: 1-4180-1166-5

Delmar Cengage Learning
5 Maxwell Drive
Clifton Park, NY 12065-2919
USA

Cengage Learning is a leading provider of customized learning solutions with office locations around the globe, including Singapore, the United Kingdom, Australia, Mexico, Brazil, and Japan. Locate your local office at: **www.cengage.com/global**

Cengage Learning products are represented in Canada by Nelson Education, Ltd.

To learn more about Delmar, visit **www.cengage.com/delmar**

Purchase any of our products at your local college store or at our preferred online store **www.ichapters.com**

Printed in Canada
4 5 6 7 8 10 09 08

TABLE OF CONTENTS

This tool was developed to help you, the budding teacher and/or child care provider, as you move into your first classroom. The editors at Delmar, a part of Cengage Learning, encourage and appreciate your feedback on this or any of our other products. Go to http://www.earlychilded.delmar.cengage.com and click on the "Professional Enhancement Series feedback" link to let us know what you think.

INTRODUCTION

Throughout a college preparation program to become an early childhood educator, students take many courses and read many textbooks. Their knowledge grows as they accumulate ideas from lectures, reading, experiences, and discussions. When they finish their coursework, graduate, and move into their first teaching positions, students often leave behind some of the books they have used. The hope is, however, that they take with them the important ideas from their classes and books as they begin their own professional practice.

More experienced colleagues or mentors sometimes support teachers in their first teaching positions, helping them make the transition from the college classroom to being responsible for a group of young children. Other times, new teachers are left to travel their own paths, relying on their own resources. Whatever your situation, this professional enhancement guide is designed to provide reminders of what you have learned, as well as resources to help you make sense of and apply that knowledge.

Teachers of young children are under great pressure today. Families demand support in their difficult tasks of child-rearing in today's fast-paced and changing world. Some families become so overwhelmed with the tasks of parenting that they seem to leave too much responsibility on the shoulders of teachers and caregivers. From administrators and institutions, there are expectations that sometimes seem overwhelming. Teachers are being held accountable for children's learning in ways unprecedented in even the recent past. Public scrutiny has led to insistence on teaching practices that may seem contrary to the best interests of children or their teachers. New teachers may find themselves caught between the realities of the schools or centers where they are working, and their own philosophies and ideals of working with children. When faced with such dilemmas, these individuals need to be able to fall back and reflect on what they know of best practices and, in so doing, renew their professional determination to make appropriate decisions for children.

This book is intended as a resource guide and a reference for issues relevant to health, safety, and nutrition. This manual is for use by child care providers, directors, and other professionals who work with programs for young children.

This professional enhancement book is one of many guides that can be helpful in effectively integrating health, safety, and nutrition into quality child care programs. No guide should be used in isolation. This book is not intended to be read from cover to cover, but instead should be used as a listing of information and sources that can be helpful to teachers of young children.

The transition from the adult academic classroom into the real world of classrooms full of young children can be difficult. The resources and information included in this book can be used as one of many tools to ease the transition from the role of adult student to the role of child care provider or teacher.

This book provides a few of the tools that will be helpful to those beginning careers as teachers of young children:

- Tips for getting off to a great start in your new environment
- Reflections for growing teachers
- Important considerations for planning quality programs
- Developmental indicators
- Suggestions for materials that promote development for children from infancy through the primary grades
- Observation and assessment tools
- Examples of appropriate activity plans for health, safety, and nutrition
- Additional suggested ideas for activity plans

- Health, safety, and nutrition resources

- Case scenarios of relevant, realistic situations you may face, as well as best practices for successfully navigating them

- Insight into issues and trends facing early childhood educators today

- Books for children and ideas for promoting literacy

- A listing of professional organizations to research or join to further your development

Becoming a teacher is a continuing process of growing, learning, reflecting, and discovering through experience. Having these resources will help you along your way. Good luck on your journey!

REFLECTIONS FOR GROWING TEACHERS

Teachers spend most of their time working with young children and their families. During the day, questions and concerns arise and decisions have to be made, meaning teachers must always be reflective about their work. Too often, teachers believe they are too busy to spend time thinking, but experienced professional teachers have learned that reflection sustains their best work. Growing teachers need to take time on a regular basis to consider the questions and concerns that arise from their practice. Some teachers use journals to keep track of the process.

Use these questions to begin your reflection and then add questions from your own experience. Remember, these are not questions to be answered once and forgotten, so come back and review them often.

QUESTIONS FOR REFLECTION

This day would have been better if _____

_____.

I think I need to know more about _____

_____.

One new thing I think I'll try this week is _____

_____.

The highlight of this week was _____

_____.

The observations this week made me think more about _____

_____.

I think my favorite creative activity this year was _____

_____.

One area where my teaching is changing is _____

_____.

One area where my teaching needs to change is _____

_____.

I just don't understand why _____

_____.

I loved my job this week when _____

_____.

I hated my job this week when _____

_____.

One thing I can try to make better next week is _____

_____.

The funniest thing I heard a child say this week was _____

_____.

The family member I feel most comfortable with is _____

_____.

And I think the reason for that is _____

_____.

The family member I feel least comfortable with is _____

_____.

And I think the reason for that is _____

_____.

The biggest gains in learning have been made by _____

_____.

And I think that this is because _____

_____.

I'm working on a bad habit of _____

_____.

Has my attitude about teaching changed this year? Why? _____

_____.

What have I done lately to spark the children's imagination and creativity? _____

_____.

One quote that I like to keep in mind is _____

_____.

Dealing with _____ is the most difficult thing I had to face recently
because _____

_____.

My teaching style has been most influenced by _____

_____.

In thinking more about health, safety, and nutrition in my curriculum, I
believe _____

_____.

If I were going to advise a new teacher, the most helpful piece of advice would
be _____

_____.

I've been trying to facilitate friendships among the children by _____

_____.

I really need to start _____

_____.

I used to _____ but now I _____

_____.

The child who has helped me learn the most is _____. I learned _____

_____.

I've grown in my communication by _____

_____.

The best thing I've learned by observing is _____

_____.

I still don't understand why _____

_____.

One mistake I used to make that I don't make any longer is _____

_____.

When next year starts, one thing I will do more of is _____

_____.

When next year starts, one thing I won't do is _____

_____.

One way I can help my children feel more competent is _____

_____.

Something I enjoy that I could share with my class is _____

_____.

When children have difficulty sharing, I _____

_____

_____

_____

_____

_____.

Adapted from Nilsen, B. A., *Week by Week: Documenting the Development of Young Children*, 3E, published by Thomson Delmar Learning.

TIPS FOR SUCCESS

Remember that you are a role model for the children. They are constantly watching how you dress, what you say, and what you do.

BE A PROFESSIONAL

- Dress conservatively and follow your employer's clothing expectations (which could include wearing closed-toe shoes to be safe and active with children and wearing clean, modest, and comfortable clothing).

- Be prepared and on time.

- Avoid excessive absences.

- Use appropriate language with children and adults.

- Be positive when talking to parents and show that you are forming a positive relationship with their children; "catch children doing something right" and share those accomplishments. Challenges with children can be discussed after you have established trust with the parents.

BE A TEAM PLAYER

- Rely on team members to help you learn the parameters of your new position.

- Don't be afraid to ask questions or request guidance from teammates.

- Show your support and be responsible.

- Step in to do your share of the work; don't expect others to clean up after you.

- Assist others whenever possible.

- Respect others' ideas and avoid telling them how to do things.

- Strive to balance your ability to make decisions with following the lead of others.

LEARN ABOUT CHILDREN

- Be aware of children's development physically, socially, emotionally, and cognitively.

- Assess children's development and plan curriculum that will enhance it.

- Be aware that children will test you! (Children, especially school age, will expect that you don't know the rules and may try to convince you to let them do things that were not previously allowed.)

- Never hesitate to double-check something with teammates when in doubt.

- Use positive management techniques with children.

GUIDANCE TECHNIQUES FOR GAINING CHILDREN'S COOPERATION

Myriad techniques are useful for helping children cooperate. Children need respectful reminders of expectations and adult support to help them perform to those expectations. Be sure that your expectations are age appropriate and individually appropriate. These techniques are more preventive in nature:

- Use positive phrases and state exactly what you expect children to do. "Stand by the door" is more effective than "Don't go outside until everyone is ready."

- Avoid "no" and "don't." Be clear about what you want children to do, not what you don't want them to do.

- Sequence your directions by using "When-then" phrasing; for example, "When things are put away where they belong, then we can go outside."

- Stay close. Merely standing near children can be enough to help them manage behavior. Be aware, however, that if you are talking to another adult, children may act out because they know they do not have your attention.

- Offer sufficient and appropriate choices. Children need a variety of activities that interest them and that will create opportunities for success.

- Create a schedule that balances children's activity with quieter periods to help children retain control.

GETTING STARTED

When starting in a new position working with children, there is always an array of information to learn. Use this fill-in-the blank section to customize this resource book to your specific environment.

What are the school's or center's hours of operation?

On school days: _____

_____

_____

On vacation days: _____

_____

_____

What is the basic daily schedule and what are my responsibilities during each time segment?

_____

_____

_____

_____

_____

_____

What are the procedures for checking children in and out of the program?

_____

_____

Do I call if I must be absent? Who is my contact?

Name:_____

Phone number: _____

What is the dress code for employees?

_____

_____

For what basic health and safety practices will I be responsible? Where are the materials stored?

Sanitizing tables: _____

_____

_____

_____

Cleaning and maintaining equipment and materials (bleach, gloves, and so on): __

_____

_____

_____

What are the emergency procedures?

Mildly injured child: _____

_____

_____

_____

_____

Earthquake/tornado: _____

_____

_____

_____

_____

_____

Fire: _____

_____

_____

_____

_____

First aid: _____

_____

_____

_____

_____

Other: _____

_____

_____

_____

_____

THE INTERRELATEDNESS OF HEALTH, SAFETY, AND NUTRITION

Any discussion of quality child care programs for young children must consider the interrelationship among health, safety, and nutrition. This relationship parallels the way in which social, emotional, cognitive, language, and physical development are interconnected. For example, the busy schedule maintained by many families often decreases the opportunity to prepare and share wholesome meals together. Therefore, a rushed diet of fast foods can negatively impact the child's heath as well as create social and emotional development implications. When teachers of young children adopt the concept that a child's health, safety, and well-being are intertwined, they can begin to build programs and the curriculum in a way that benefits the child and the family. All programs should strive toward four main goals:

1. Maximize the health of young children.

2. Minimize the risks for children.

3. Maintain guidelines and regulations.

4. Maximize educational opportunities for children and families. (Robertson, p. 21)

As with any aspect of development, a child does not live and grow in a vacuum. The child's environment is composed of physical factors, economic factors, social factors, emotional factors, and cultural influences. Each of these components is a vital part of the holistic environment for the child. To understand this interrelationship, think of a time when you were very stressed. Was your diet altered? Did you feel more fatigued? Were you less able to concentrate? Did you find yourself more prone to confusion and to accidents? In the same way, when families and children are stressed, their health, safety, and nutrition are adversely affected. The families' cultural patterns might also play a part in how stress is handled.

New teachers must view families as partners in the implementation of healthy and safe programs for young children. Keep the lines of communication open. Learn about children from their families and share resource materials and information with parents in an effort to help them understand the important part that the family plays in maintaining the health, safety, and nutrition of their children.

Use the Join Us in Our Journey of Successful Living letter template (Figure 1) to encourage parents and others to get involved with successful living.

Join Us in Our Journey of Successful Living!

Date: _____

Dear _____,

HELP US TO MAXIMIZE A CHILD'S POTENTIAL!

The good health of your child is very important to us. Among the many objectives we will focus on this school year will be maximizing the child's potential through the knowledge of how important health, safety, and nutrition concepts are for all people regardless of age.

We are studying the importance of making informed choices that will impact the growth and development of children. Please discuss the topics of the week, listed below, with your child(ren) to further reinforce learning outcomes. We also ask that you complete the following questionnaire so that we can better support you and your family. Thank you in advance for your support and participation.

_____

_____

_____

_____

_____

_____

_____

_____

_____

_____

_____

Sincerely,

_____

Figure 1

Mindful of Maximizing a Child's Potential

Questionnaire

1. Do you place emphasis on eating healthy?   Yes   No   Somewhat

2. If so, please share at least one way you emphasize eating healthy. _____

_____

_____

_____

3. Are there barriers to eating healthy?   Yes   No   Somewhat

4. If so, please list some of these barriers. _____

_____

_____

_____

5. Are there specific ways the center/school could assist you in learning more about making healthier choices when selecting foods for meals? _____

_____

_____

_____

6. Are you available as well as interested in volunteering in our class to help promote healthy choices?   Yes   No

7. If so, please select those activities of interest to you:

   o Reading stories to the class that promote health, safety, and nutrition concepts

   o Sending in supplies for activities that promote health, safety, and nutrition concepts

   o Charting examples of promoting healthy choices outside of school time

   o Participating in a weekly exercise activity

   o Other suggestions: _____

Figure 1 *continued*

ASSESSMENT AND OBSERVATION TOOLS FOR HEALTH

The important considerations in planning for healthy programs include the following:

- Health components of the program should be carefully planned with comprehensive policies that are enforced in an effort to protect the children and those who work with them.

- All staff members should understand the importance of maintaining the health of young children and take responsibility for their part in the process.

- Families should be included as an integral part of the health education program.

- Programs should focus on the prevention of illnesses.

- Teachers should be good models of healthy practices.

- The program should educate children, faculty, and families about healthy life styles.

- Universal precautions for handling bodily fluids should be observed by all.

DEVELOPMENTAL MILESTONES

As with any aspect of working with young children, teachers must understand the typical sequence of developmental indicators so that appropriate expectations are in place. When considering health issues, it is important to begin by examining some of the major developmental milestones of young children. Table 1 gives an overview of some of the developmental milestones.

TABLE 1   Major Developmental Achievements

Age	Achievements
2 months	lifts head up when placed on stomach
	follows moving person or object with eyes
	imitates or responds to smiling person with occasional smiles
	turns toward source of sound
	begins to make simple sounds and noises
	grasps objects with entire hand; not strong enough to hold on
	enjoys being held and cuddled
4 months	has good control of head
	reaches for and grasps objects with both hands
	laughs out loud; vocalizes with coos and giggles
	waves arms about
	holds head erect when supported in a sitting position
	rolls over from side to back to stomach
	recognizes familiar objects (e.g., bottle, toy)
6 months	grasps objects with entire hand; transfers objects from one hand to the other and from hand to mouth
	sits alone with minimal support
	deliberately reaches for, grasps, and holds objects
	plays games and imitates (e.g., peek-a-boo)
	shows signs of teeth beginning to erupt
	prefers primary caregiver to strangers
	babbles using different sounds
	raises up and supports weight of upper body on arms
9 months	sits alone; able to maintain balance while changing positions
	picks up objects with pincer grasp (first finger and thumb)
	begins to crawl
	attempts to say words such as "mama" and "dada"
	is hesitant toward strangers
	explores new objects by chewing or placing them in mouth
12 months	pulls up to a standing position
	may "walk" by holding on to objects
	stacks several objects one on top of the other
	responds to simple commands and own name
	babbles using jargon in sentence-like form
	uses hands, eyes, and mouth to investigate new objects
	can hold own eating utensils

(continued)

TABLE 1   Major Developmental Achievements (Continued)

Age	Achievements
18 months	crawls up and down stairs one at a time
	walks unassisted; has difficulty avoiding obstacles in pathway
	is less fearful of strangers
	enjoys being read to; likes toys for pushing and pulling
	has a vocabulary consisting of approximately 5 to 50 words, can name familiar objects
	helps feed self; manages spoon and cup
2 years	runs, walks with ease; can kick and throw a ball; jumps in place
	speaks in two- to three-word sentences; asks simple questions; knows about 200 words
	displays parallel play
	achieves daytime toilet training
	voices displeasure
3 years	climbs stairs using alternating feet
	can hop and balance on one foot
	feeds self
	can help dress and undress; washes own hands and brushes teeth with help
	is usually toilet trained
	is curious; asks and answers questions
	enjoys drawing, cutting with scissors, painting, playing with clay, and playing make-believe
	can throw and bounce a ball
	states name; recognizes self in pictures
4 years	dresses and undresses self; helps with bathing; manages own tooth brushing
	enjoys creative activities: paints, draws with detail, models with clay, builds imaginative structures with blocks
	rides a bike with confidence, turns corners, maintains balance
	climbs, runs, and hops with skill and vigor
	enjoys friendships and playing with small groups of children
	enjoys and seeks adult approval
	understands simple concepts (e.g., shortest, longest, same)
5 years	expresses ideas and questions clearly and with fluency
	has vocabulary consisting of approximately 2,500 to 3,000 words

(*continued*)

TABLE 1   Major Developmental Achievements (Continued)

Age	Achievements
5 years	substitutes verbal for physical expressions of displeasure
	dresses without supervision
	seeks reassurance and recognition for achievements
	engages in active and energetic play, especially outdoors
	throws and catches a ball with relative accuracy
	cuts with scissors along a straight line; draws in detail
6 years	plays with enthusiasm and vigor
	develops increasing interest in books and reading
	displays greater independence from adults; makes fewer requests for help
	forms close friendships with several peers
	exhibits improved motor skills; can jump rope, hop and skip, ride a bicycle
	enjoys conversation
	sorts objects by color and shape
7 and 8 years	enjoys friends; seeks their approval
	shows increased curiosity and interest in exploration
	develops greater clarity of gender identity
	is motivated by a sense of achievement
	begins to reveal a moral consciousness

Adapted from Allen K. E., & Marotz, L. R. (2003). *Developmental profiles* (4th ed.). Clifton Park, NY: Thomson Delmar Learning.

Middle childhood is another important transition in a child's life. Many changes are occurring with this age group. Reference the following chart to assist you in supporting the school-age child.

Developmental Achievement for the School-Age Child 5–6

Physical

- Growth slows down
- Prefers to play over group games
- Enjoys and needs physical activity
- Gross motor skills are increasing, but there are limits to what the child can do
- Fine motor skills are still developing, but good progress is evident (writing, cutting, snapping fingers)

Cognitive & Language

- Capable of responding to and asking questions
- Ability to reason increases, but concrete examples are needed
- Can problem solve
- Active learning is needed
- Attention span is limited
- Beginning to learn letters and associate sounds
- Sight word recognition

Social

- Forms friendships, may have a new best friend often
- Competitive games are difficult
- Beginning to identify with others
- Beginning to enjoy jokes
- Enjoys working in small groups

Emotional

- Can be easily offended
- Desires praise from others
- Fears are common
- Enjoys helping others and the way it makes him or her feel
- Failure to win all games/activities can pose a problem

Developmental Achievement for the School-Age Child 7—9

Physical

- Growth consistent
- Good coordination
- Enjoys playing games
- High energy
- Works to master physical activities and sports
- Fine and gross motor skills are increasing

Cognitive & Language

- Uses learning strategies to complete and master skills and new knowledge
- Capable of distinguishing similarities and differences
- Abstract thinking begins, but concrete supports are needed
- More use of language to express ideas

Cognitive & Language, continued

- Can make plans and carry them out
- May experiment with slang or profanity

Social

- Talkative
- Develops friendship/shares secrets/usually the same gender
- Moral development begins
- Will make value judgments concerning behaviors and situations
- Becoming independent and outgoing
- Still eager to please

Emotional

- Criticism can cause concerns for the child
- Hates to be teased
- Eager to learn
- Concerned about failure
- May avoid participating to avoid failure
- Increased need to argue

HEALTH ASSESSMENTS

One of the keys to maintaining the health of young children is to develop the practice of conducting brief daily assessments of young children. Through careful observation skills, the teacher can quickly recognize some possible health problems. Teachers should pay close attention to children's general appearance, scalp, face, eyes, ears, nose, mouth, throat, neck check, skin, speech, extremities, and behavioral indicators. Table 2 explains exactly what types of things should be observed in each of these areas.

TABLE 2   Health Observation Checklist

1. *General appearance*—note changes in weight (gain or loss), signs of fatigue or unusual excitability, skin tone (pallor or flushed), and size for age group.
2. *Scalp*—observe for signs of itching, head lice, sores, hair loss, and cleanliness.
3. *Face*—notice general expression (e.g., fear, anger, happy, anxious), skin tone, and any scratches, bruises, or rashes.

4. *Eyes*—look for redness, tearing, puffiness, sensitivity to light, frequent rubbing, sties, sores, drainage, or uncoordinated eye movements.

5. *Ears*—check for drainage, redness, and appropriate responses to sounds or verbal requests.

6. *Nose*—note any deformity, frequent rubbing, congestion, sneezing, or drainage.

7. *Mouth*—look inside at the teeth; note cavities, malformations, sores, or mouth-breathing.

8. *Throat*—observe for enlarged or red tonsils, red throat, white patches on throat or tonsils, drainage, or unusual breath odors.

9. *Neck*—feel for enlarged glands.

10. *Chest*—watch the child's breathing and note any wheezing, rattles, shortness of breath, coughing (with or without other symptoms).

11. *Skin*—lift up clothing and observe the chest and back for color (pallor or redness), rashes, scratches, bumps, bruises, scars, unusual warmth, and perspiration.

12. *Speech*—listen for clarity, stuttering, nasality, mispronunciations, monotone voice, and appropriateness for age.

13. *Extremities*—observe posture, coordination; note conditions such as bowed legs, toeing-in, or arms and legs of unequal length.

14. *Behavior and temperament*—note any changes in activity level, alertness, cooperation, appetite, sleep patterns, toileting habits, irritability, or uncharacteristic restlessness.

Reprinted with permission, *Health, Safety, and Nutrition for the Young Child*, Marotz, Cross, and Rush, 2005. Thomson Delmar Learning.

Proper Procedures for Taking Temperatures

One of the most common procedures performed by teachers to monitor the health of children is taking temperatures. Temperatures are traditionally taken in several basic ways: oral, rectal, axillary (underarm), and aural (ear canal). Note that to take rectal or aural temperatures, some additional training is needed to avoid harming the child who might be moving or distressed.

When taking temperatures with young children, the glass mercury thermometers are considered unsafe. The digital or infrared thermometers are the best choices. Thermometers must also be used in a sanitary way. There are two sanitation procedures. Teachers may use a disposal plastic sheath, or the thermometer may be wiped with alcohol or washed with soap and cool water. Follow the cleaning suggestions given by the manufacturer of the particular thermometer used.

Table 3 gives some instructions on taking different types of temperatures.

TABLE 3　Taking a Child's Temperature

Axillary (underarm)	Place a clean oral thermometer under a dry arm of the child.
	Hold the child's arm gently against chest for about 5 minutes.
Rectal (must use rectal thermometer only)	This technique is not suggested for children younger than two months or older than two years.
	Place the child on his or her stomach.
	Lubricate the anal area and the end of the thermometer.
	Do not insert the thermometer more than ¾ inch.
	Gently hold the buttocks together, being careful not to push the thermometer further.
	Wait with the child for about 2 or 3 minutes while taking the temperature.
Oral	Make sure that the child has not had anything to drink in the past 15 minutes.
	Put the end of the thermometer under the side of the tongue.
	Make sure that the child holds the thermometer in place with lips instead of teeth.
	Wait with the child for about 3 minutes while taking the temperature.

Proper Hand Washing

Teachers should remember that the best way to cut down on the spread of germs in any setting is frequent and proper hand washing by all children and staff in the classroom. During certain crucial times of the day, hand washing should be stressed. The following is a list of activities that necessitate hand washing:

- Entry into the classroom at the beginning of the day

- Before handling food or food utensils

- Before and after eating

- Before and after giving medications, taking temperatures

- Before and after using the water table with another child

- After using the toilet, diapering a child, or assisting a child with toileting

- After touching animals

- After playing in sand or other similar material

- After handling raw foods

- After emptying the trash

Everyone should wash hands properly and frequently according to the following directions:

1. Use liquid soap and warm running water.

2. Rub hand on all sides for 10 seconds (the amount of time needed to sing Happy Birthday).

3. Wash the backs of hands.

4. Wash the wrists.

5. Wash between fingers.

6. Wash under fingernails (a small brush works well).

7. Rinse well under warm running water.

8. Dry hand with a paper towel.

9. Use the paper towel to turn off the faucet.

Universal Precautions

Many times, teachers of young children come into contact with bodily fluids. Safe guidelines for handling bodily fluids must always be observed every time bodily fluid is handled. It does not matter how well the teacher knows the child or the child's family. The same safe procedures should be used always. Table 4 explains the basic procedures.

TABLE 4   Universal Precautions for Handling Body Fluids

- Wear disposable latex gloves when you are likely to have contact with blood or other body fluids, for example, vomit, urine, feces, or saliva.
- Remove glove by grasping the cuff and pulling it off inside out.
- Wash hands thoroughly (lather for approximately 30 seconds).
- Dispose of contaminated materials properly. Seal soiled clothing in plastic bags to be laundered at home. Dispose of diapers by tying them securely in garbage bags. Place broken glass in a designated container.

(continued)

TABLE 4   Universal Precautions for Handling Body Fluids (Continued)

- Clean all surfaces with a disinfectant, such as a bleach solution (1 tablespoon bleach/1 cup water mixed fresh daily).
- Subsidize the cost of hepatitis B immunizations for all employees.

Reprinted with permission, *Health, Safety, and Nutrition for the Young Child,* Marotz, Cross, and Rush, 2005. Thomson Delmar Learning.

Proper Sanitation Practices

In addition to proper hand washing and the observation of universal precautions, several other factors are important to maintaining a healthy environment for young children. Regularly sanitizing items and surfaces in the classroom is important. Proper diapering procedures must be part of the regular routine.

For all surfaces to be effectively sanitized, a proper strength of bleach solution must be used regularly. Following are the proper procedures for mixing bleach solution:

1. Remember that bleach solution must be mixed fresh every day to effectively kill germs.

2. Mix 1 tablespoon of bleach for 1 quart of water. Mark a line on the plastic spray bottle for the level of each to save time.

3. Make sure surfaces are clean before they are disinfected with the bleach solution.

4. Make sure that the entire surface is sprayed lightly.

5. Leave the solution on the surface for 2 minutes before drying it with a paper towel. Air drying is also acceptable.

6. Always keep the bleach solution out of reach of children.

Diaper Changing Procedures

Diaper changing can be a special challenge for sanitation. The following information outlines the suggested procedure for changing diapers.

1. Make sure that all supplies are ready and easily accessible.

2. Place a disposable towel on the diapering surface.

3. Lay the child on the diapering surface and make sure there is no danger of the child rolling off.

4. Remove soiled diaper and clothing; place disposable diapers in a receptacle lined with plastic and place soiled clothing in a plastic bag.

5. Use either a premoistened towelette or a damp paper towel to clean the child's bottom.

6. Dispose of the towel in a plastic bag or a receptacle lined with plastic.

7. Remove the paper liner from under the child and dispose of it in the same way.

8. Wipe your hands with a damp paper towel and dispose of it in the plastic bag or plastic-lined receptacle.

9. Diaper or dress the child.

10. Wash the child's hands and return the child to the group.

11. Clean and disinfect the diapering areas and any supplies that you might have touched.

12. Wash your hands.

13. Remember that in addition to compiling with the sanitation guidelines, diapering times should also be used as learning opportunities and nurturing times for young children. Diapering time is a good time to do songs and chants with the children as they are being changed. The children will enjoy it and you will be amazed by how it changes the experience for you as well.

Regular Cleaning and Sanitation

To insure the proper sanitation of the environment, you should establish a regular routine of cleaning and sanitizing materials and areas in the classroom. Some of the crucial areas to clean regularly include counters, tables, carpets, utensils, toys, sleeping items, cribs, telephones, toileting/diapering areas, sinks, and waste containers. Refer to Table 5 for a better understanding of how to maintain materials and surfaces appropriately.

Communicable Illnesses

To protect children from disease and illnesses, teachers must understand the various types of communicable diseases and the method of transmission as well as the best ways to control the spread of diseases. Table 6 can help teachers understand diseases, what symptoms to look for, and how to best control the spread of illnesses.

TABLE 5   Routine Frequency of Cleaning and Sanitation Checklist

Area	Clean	Sanitize	Frequency
Classrooms/Child Care/Food Areas			
Countertops/tabletops, floors, door and cabinet handles	X	X	Daily and when soiled.
Food preparation & service surfaces	X	X	Before and after contact with food activity; between preparation of raw and cooked foods.
Carpets and large area rugs	X		Vacuum daily when children are not present. Clean with a carpet cleaning method approved by the local health authority. Clean carpets only when children will not be present until the carpet is dry. Clean carpets at least monthly in infant areas, at least every 3 months in other areas and when soiled.
Small rugs	X		Shake outdoors or vacuum daily. Launder weekly.
Utensils, surfaces, and toys that go into the mouth or have been in contact with saliva or other body fluids	X	X	After each child's use, or use disposable, one-time utensils or toys.
Toys that are not contaminated with body fluids. Dress-up clothes not worn on the head. Sheets and pillowcases, individual cloth towels (if used), combs and hairbrushes, wash cloth and machine-washable cloth toys. (None of these items should be shared among children.)	X		Weekly and when visibly soiled.
Blankets, sleeping bags, cubbies	X		Monthly and when soiled.
Hats	X		After each child's use or use disposable hats that only one child wears.
Cribs and crib mattresses	X		Weekly, before use by a different child, and whenever soiled or wet.
Phone receivers	X	X	Weekly.

Area	Clean	Sanitize	Frequency
Toilet and Diapering Areas			
Hand-washing sinks, faucets, surrounding Counters, soap dispensers, door knobs	X	X	Daily and when soiled.
Toilet seats, toilet handles, door knobs or cubicle handles, floors	X	X	Daily, or immediately if visibly soiled.
Toilet bowls	X	X	Daily.
Changing tables, potty chairs (use of potty chairs in child care is discouraged because of high risk of contamination)	X	X	After each child's use.
General Facility			
Mops and cleaning rags	X	X	Before and after a day of use, wash mops and rags in detergent and water, rinse in water, immerse in sanitizing solution, and wring as dry as possible. After cleaning and sanitizing, hang mops and rags to dry.
Waste and diaper containers	X		Daily.
Any surface contaminated with body fluids: saliva, mucus, vomit, urine, stool, or blood	X	X	Immediately, as specified in Standard 3.026.

Source: Keeping Healthy, NAEYC brochure, 1999.
Reprinted with permission, NAEYC.

Immunization Schedule

An important responsibility of parents and of child care centers is to insure that all children have up-to-date immunizations. Through the process of universal immunizations, the incidence of certain serious diseases can be avoided. Refer to Table 7 to see the schedule for childhood immunizations.

Administering Medications

Many times, children have prescription medicine that they need to take after they return to the child care program or school. No medications should be given to a child unless the medicine is prescribed by a doctor and is labeled accordingly. All medicines must be stored properly in a locked container, and proper documentation must be maintained when medicine is administered. Table 8 gives general guidelines and suggestions for administering medications to children.

TABLE 6   Common Communicable Illnesses

Communicable Illness	Signs and Symptoms	Infectious Agent	Methods of Transmission	Incubation Period	Length of Communicability	Control Measures
AIRBORNE TRANSMITTED ILLNESS						
Chickenpox	Slight fever, irritability, cold-like symptoms. Red rash that develops blister-like head, scabs later. Most abundant on covered parts of body, e.g., chest, back, neck, forearm.	Virus	Airborne through contact with secretions from the respiratory tract. Transmission from contact with blisters less common.	2–3 weeks after exposure	2–3 days prior to the onset of symptoms until 5–6 days after first eruptions. Scabs are not contagious.	Specific control measures: (1) Exclusion of sick children, (2) Practice good personal hygiene, especially careful hand washing. Children can return to group care when all blisters have formed a dry scab (approximately 1 week). Immunization is now available.
Common Cold	Highly contagious infection of the upper respiratory tract accompanied by slight fever, chills, runny nose, fatigue, muscle and headaches. Onset may be sudden.	Virus	Airborne through contact with secretions from the respiratory tract, e.g., coughs, sneezes, eating utensils, etc.	12–72 hours	About 1 day before onset of symptoms to 2–3 days after acute illness.	Prevention through education and good personal hygiene. Avoid exposure. Exclude first day or two. Antibiotics not effective against viruses. Avoid aspirin products (possible link to Reye's syndrome). Watch for complications, e.g., earaches, bronchitis, croup, pneumonia.

(continued)

TABLE 6   Common Communicable Illnesses (Continued)

Communicable Illness	Signs and Symptoms	Infectious Agent	Methods of Transmission	Incubation Period	Length of Communicability	Control Measures
Fifth's disease	Appearance of bright red rash on face, especially cheeks.	Virus	Airborne contact with secretions from the nose/mouth of infected person.	4–14 days	Prior to appearance of rash; probably not after rash develops.	Don't need to exclude children once rash appears. Frequent hand washing; frequent washing/disinfecting of toys/surfaces. Use care when handling tissues/nasal secretions.
Haemophilus influenza Type b	An acute respiratory infection; frequently causes meningitis. Other complications include pneumonia, epiglottitis, arthritis, infections of the bloodstream and conjunctivitis.	Bacteria	Airborne via secretions of the respiratory tract (nose, throat). Persons can also be carriers with or without symptoms.	2–4 days	Throughout acute phase; as long as organism is present. Noncommunicable 36–48 hours after treatment with antibiotics.	Identify and exclude sick children. Treatment with antibiotics 3–4 days before returning to group care. Notify parents of exposed children to contact their physician. Immunize children. Practice good hand-washing techniques; sanitize contaminated objects.
Measles (Rubeola)	Fever, cough, runny nose, eyes sensitive to light. Dark red blotchy rash that often begins on the face and neck, then spreads over the entire body. Highly communicable.	Virus	Airborne through coughs, sneezes and contact with contaminated articles.	8–13 days; rash develops approximately 14 days after exposure	From beginning of symptoms until 4 days after rash appears.	Most effective control method is immunization. Good personal hygiene, especially hand washing and covering the mouth when coughing. Exclude child for at least 4 days after rash appears.

(continued)

OUACHITA TECHNICAL COLLEGE

TABLE 6   Common Communicable Illnesses (Continued)

Communicable Illness	Signs and Symptoms	Infectious Agent	Methods of Transmission	Incubation Period	Length of Communicability	Control Measures
Meningitis	Sudden onset of fever, stiff neck, headache, irritability, and vomiting; gradual loss of consciousness, seizures, and death.	Bacteria	Airborne through coughs, nasal secretions; direct contact with saliva/ nasal discharges.	Varies with the infecting organism; 2–4 days average	Throughout acute phase; noncommunicable after antibiotic treatment.	Encourage immunization for Exclude child from care until medical treatment is completed. Use Universal Precautions when handling saliva/nasal secretions, frequent hand washing, and disinfecting of toys/surfaces.
Mononucleosis	Characteristic symptoms include sore throat, intermittent fever, fatigue, and enlarged lymph glands in the neck. May also be accompanied by headache and enlarged liver or spleen.	Virus	Airborne; also direct contact with saliva of an infected person.	2–4 weeks for children; 4–6 weeks for adults	Unknown. Organisms may be present in oral secretions for as long as one year following illness.	None known. Child should be kept home until over the acute phase (6–10 days). Use frequent handwashing and careful disposal of tissues after coughing or blowing nose.
Mumps	Sudden onset of fever with swelling of the salivary glands.	Virus	Airborne through coughs and sneezes; direct contact with oral secretions of infected persons.	12–26 days	6–7 days prior to the onset of symptoms until swelling in the salivary glands is gone (7–9 days).	Immunization provides permanent protection. Peak incidence is in winter and spring. Exclude children from school or group settings until all symptoms have disappeared.

(continued)

TABLE 6   Common Communicable Illnesses (Continued)

Communicable Illness	Signs and Symptoms	Infectious Agent	Methods of Transmission	Incubation Period	Length of Communicability	Control Measures
Roseola Infantum (6–24 mo.)	Most common in the spring and fall. Fever rises abruptly (102°–105°F) and lasts 3–4 days; loss of appetite, listlessness, runny nose, rash on trunk, arms, and neck lasting 1–2 days.	Virus	Person to person; method unknown.	10–15 days	1–2 days before onset to several days following fading of the rash.	Exclude from school or group care until rash and fever are gone.
Rubella (German measles)	Mild fever; rash begins on face and neck and rarely lasts more than 3 days. May have arthritis-like discomfort and swelling in joints.	Virus	Airborne through contact with respiratory secretions, e.g., coughs, sneezes.	4–21 days	From one week prior to 5 days following onset of the rash.	Immunization offers permanent protection. Children must be excluded from school for at least 7 days after appearance of rash.

(continued)

TABLE 6 Common Communicable Illnesses (Continued)

Communicable Illness	Signs and Symptoms	Infectious Agent	Methods of Transmission	Incubation Period	Length of Communicability	Control Measures
Streptococcal Infections (strep throat, scarlatina, rheumatic fever)	Sudden, onset. High fever accompanied by sore, red throat; may also have nausea, vomiting, headache, white patches on tonsils, and enlarged glands. Development of a rash depends on the infectious organism.	Bacteria	Airborne via droplets from coughs or sneezes. May also be transmitted by food and raw milk.	1–4 days	Throughout the illness and for approximately 10 days afterward, unless treated with antibiotics. Medical treatment eliminates communicability within 36 hours. Can develop rheumatic fever or become a carrier if not treated.	Exclude child with symptoms. Antibiotic treatment is essential. Avoid crowding in classrooms. Practice frequent hand washing, educating children, and careful supervision of food handlers.
Tuberculosis	Many people have no symptoms. Active disease causes productive cough, weight loss, fatigue, loss of appetite, chills, night sweats.	Bacteria	Airborne via coughs or sneezes.	2–3 months	As long as disease is untreated; usually noncontagious after 2–3 weeks on medication.	TB skin testing, especially babies and young children, if there has been contact with an infected person. Seek prompt diagnosis and treatment if experiencing symptoms; complete drug therapy. Cover coughs/sneezes. Practice good hand washing.

(continued)

TABLE 6   Common Communicable Illnesses (Continued)

Communicable Illness	Signs and Symptoms	Infectious Agent	Methods of Transmission	Incubation Period	Length of Communicability	Control Measures
BLOOD BORNE TRANSMITTED ILLNESSES						
Acquired Immuno-deficiency Syndrome (AIDS)	Flu-like symptoms, including fatigue, weight loss, enlarged lymph glands, persistent cough, fever, and diarrhea.	Virus	Children acquire virus when born to infected mothers from contaminated blood transfusions and possibly from breast milk of infected mothers. Adults acquire the virus via sexual transmission, contaminated drug needles, and blood transfusions.	6 weeks to 8 years	Lifetime	Exclude children 0–5 yrs. if they have open lesions, uncontrollable nosebleeds, bloody diarrhea, or are at high risk for exposing others to blood-contaminated body fluids. Use Universal Precautions when handling body fluids, including good hand-washing techniques. Seal contaminated items, e.g., diapers, paper towels in plastic bags. Disinfect surfaces with bleach/water solution (1:10) or other disinfectant.
Hepatitis B	Slow onset; loss of appetite, nausea, vomiting, abdominal pain, and jaundice. May also be **asymptomatic.**	Virus	Through contact with blood/body fluids containing blood.	45–180 days; average 60–80 days	Varies; some persons are lifetime carriers.	Immunization is preferable. Use Universal Precautions when handling any blood/ body fluids; use frequent hand washing.

(continued)

asymptomatic—*having no symptoms.*

TABLE 6   Common Communicable Illnesses (Continued)

Communicable Illness	Signs and Symptoms	Infectious Agent	Methods of Transmission	Incubation Period	Length of Communicability	Control Measures
CONTACT (direct and indirect) TRANSMITTED ILLNESSES						
Conjunctivitis (Pinkeye)	Redness of the white portion (conjunctiva) of the eye and inner eyelid, swelling of the lids, yellow discharge from eyes and itching.	Bacteria or virus	Direct contact with discharge from eyes or upper respiratory tract of an infected person; through contaminated fingers and objects, e.g., tissues, washcloths, towels.	1–3 days	Throughout active infection; several days up to 2–3 weeks.	Antibiotic treatment. Exclude child for 24 hours after medication is started. Frequent hand washing and disinfection of toys/surfaces is necessary.
Cytomegalovirus (CMV)	Often no symptoms in children under 2 yrs.; sore throat, fever, fatigue in older children. High risk of fetal damage if mother is infected during pregnancy.	Virus	Person to person contact with body fluids, e.g., saliva, blood, urine, breast milk, in utero.	Unknown; may be 4–8 weeks	Virus present (in saliva, urine) for months following infection.	No need to exclude children. Always wash hands after changing diapers or contact with saliva. Avoid kissing children's mouths or sharing eating utensils. Practice careful hand washing with children; wash/disinfect toys and surfaces frequently.

(continued)

TABLE 6   Common Communicable Illnesses (Continued)

Communicable Illness	Signs and Symptoms	Infectious Agent	Methods of Transmission	Incubation Period	Length of Communicability	Control Measures
Hand, foot, and mouth disease	Affects children under 10 yrs. Onset of fever, followed by blistered sores in the mouth/cheeks; 1–2 days later raised rash appears on palms of hands and soles of feet.	Virus	Person to person through direct contact with saliva, nasal discharge, or feces.	3–6 days	7–10 days	Exclude sick children for several days. Practice frequent hand washing, especially after changing diapers. Clean/disinfect surfaces.
Herpes simplex (Cold sores)	Clear blisters develop on face, lips, and other body parts that crust and heal within a few days	Virus	Direct contact with saliva, on hands, or sexual contact.	Up to 2 weeks	Virus remains in saliva for as long as 7 weeks following recovery.	No specific control. Frequent hand washing. Child does not have to be excluded from school.
Impetigo	Infection of the skin forming crusty, moist lesions usually on the face, ears, and around the nose. Highly contagious. Common among children.	Bacteria	Direct contact with discharge from sores; indirect contact with contaminated articles of clothing, tissues, etc.	2–5 days; may be as long as 10 days	Until lesions are healed.	Exclude from group settings until lesions have been treated with antibiotics for 24–48 hours. Cover areas with bandage until treated.

(continued)

TABLE 6   Common Communicable Illnesses (Continued)

Communicable Illness	Signs and Symptoms	Infectious Agent	Methods of Transmission	Incubation Period	Length of Communicability	Control Measures
Lice (head)	Lice are seldom visible to the naked eye. White nits (eggs) are visible on hair shafts. The most obvious symptom is itching of the scalp, especially behind the ears and at the base of the neck.	Head louse	Direct contact with infected persons or with their personal articles, e.g., hats, hair brushes, combs, or clothing. Lice can survive for 2–3 weeks on bedding, carpet, furniture, car seats, clothing, etc.	Nits hatch in 1 week and reach maturity within 8–10 days	While lice remain alive on infested persons or clothing; until nits have been destroyed	Infested children should be excluded from group settings until treated. Hair should be washed with a special medicated shampoo and rinsed with a vinegar/water solution (any concentration will work) to ease removal of all nits (using a fine-toothed comb). Heat from a hair dryer also helps destroy eggs. All friends and family should be carefully checked. Thoroughly clean child's environment; vacuum carpets/upholstery, wash/dry or dry clean bedding, clothing, hair-brushes. Seal nonwashable items in plastic bag for 2 weeks.

(continued)

TABLE 6   Common Communicable Illnesses (Continued)

Communicable Illness	Signs and Symptoms	Infectious Agent	Methods of Transmission	Incubation Period	Length of Communicability	Control Measures
Ringworm	An infection of the scalp, skin, or nails. Causes flat, spreading, oval-shaped lesions that may become dry and scaly or moist and crusted. When it is present on the feet it is commonly called athlete's foot. Infected nails may become discolored, brittle, or chalky or they may disintegrate.	Fungus	Direct or indirect contact with infected persons, their personal items, showers, swimming pools, theater seats, etc. Dogs and cats may also be infected and transmit it to children or adults.	4–10 days, (unknown for athlete's foot)	As long as lesions are present.	Exclude children from gyms, pools, or activities where they are likely to expose others. May return to group care following medical treatment with a fungicidal ointment. All shared areas, such as pools and showers should be thoroughly cleansed with a fungicide.

(continued)

TABLE 6   Common Communicable Illnesses (Continued)

Communicable Illness	Signs and Symptoms	Infectious Agent	Methods of Transmission	Incubation Period	Length of Communicability	Control Measures
Rocky Mountain spotted fever	Onset usually abrupt; fever (101°–104°F); joint and muscle pain, severe nausea and vomiting, and white coating on tongue. Rash appears on 2nd to 5th day over forehead, wrist, and ankles; later covers entire body. Can be fatal if untreated.	Bacteria	Indirect transmission: tick bite.	2–14 days; average 7 days	Not contagious from person to person.	Prompt removal of ticks; not all ticks cause illness. Administration of antibiotics. Use insect repellent on clothes when outdoors.
Scabies	Characteristic burrows or linear tunnels under the skin, especially between the fingers and around the wrists, elbows, waist, thighs, and buttocks. Causes intense itching.	Parasite	Direct contact with an infected person.	Several days to 2–4 weeks	Until all mites and eggs are destroyed.	Children should be excluded from school or group care until treated. Affected persons should bathe with prescribed soap and carefully launder all bedding and clothing. All contacts of the infected person should be notified.

(continued)

TABLE 6 Common Communicable Illnesses (Continued)

Communicable Illness	Signs and Symptoms	Infectious Agent	Methods of Transmission	Incubation Period	Length of Communicability	Control Measures
Tetanus	Muscular spasms and stiffness, especially in the muscles around the neck and mouth. Can lead to convulsions, inability to breathe, and death.	Bacteria	Indirect: organisms live in soil and dust; enter body through wounds, especially puncture-type injuries, burns and unnoticed cuts.	4 days to 2 weeks	Not contagious.	Immunization every 8–10 years affords complete protection.
FECAL/ORAL TRANSMITTED ILLNESSES						
Dysentery (Shigellosis)	Sudden onset of vomiting; diarrhea, may be accompanied by high fever, headache, abdominal pain. Stools may contain blood, pus or mucus. Can be fatal in young children.	Bacteria	Fecal-oral transmission via contaminated objects or indirectly through ingestion of contaminated food or water and via flies.	1–7 days	Variable; may last up to 4 weeks or longer in the carrier state.	Exclude child during acute illness. Careful hand washing after bowel movements. Proper disposal of human feces; control of flies. Strict adherence to sanitary procedures for food preparation.
E. coli	Diarrhea, often bloody	Bacteria	Spread through contaminated food, dirty hands.	3–4 days; can be as long as 10 days	For duration of diarrhea; usually several days.	Exclude infected children until no diarrhea; practice frequent hand washing, especially after toileting and before preparing food.

(continued)

TABLE 6   Common Communicable Illnesses (Continued)

Communicable Illness	Signs and Symptoms	Infectious Agent	Methods of Transmission	Incubation Period	Length of Communicability	Control Measures
Encephalitis	Sudden onset of headache, high fever, convulsions, vomiting, confusion, neck and back stiffness, tremors, and coma.	Virus	Indirect spread by bites from disease-carrying mosquitoes; in some areas transmitted by tick bites.	5–15 days	Humans are not contagious	Spraying of mosquito breeding areas and use of insect repellents; public education.
Giardiasis	Many persons are asymptomatic. Typical symptoms include chronic diarrhea, abdominal cramping, bloating, pale and foul-smelling stools, weight loss, and fatigue.	Parasite (protozoa)	Fecal-oral transmission; through contact with infected stool (e.g., diaper changes, helping child with soiled underwear), poor hand washing, passed from hands to mouth (toys, food). Also transmitted through contaminated water sources.	7–10 days average; can be as long as 5–25 days	As long as parasite is present in the stool.	Exclude children until diarrhea ends. Scrupulous hand washing before eating, preparing food, and after using the bathroom. Maintain sanitary conditions in bathroom areas.

(continued)

TABLE 6   Common Communicable Illnesses (Continued)

Communicable Illness	Signs and Symptoms	Infectious Agent	Methods of Transmission	Incubation Period	Length of Communicability	Control Measures
Hepatitis (Infectious; Type A)	Fever, fatigue, loss of appetite, nausea abdominal pain (in region of liver). Illness may be accompanied by yellowing of the skin and eyeballs (jaundice) in adults, but not always in children. Acute onset.	Virus	Fecal-oral route. Also spread via contaminated food, water, milk, and objects.	10–50 days (average range 25–30 days)	7–10 days prior to onset of symptoms to not more than 7 days after onset of jaundice.	Exclude from group settings a minimum of 1 week following onset. Special attention to careful hand washing after going to the bathroom and before eating is critical following an outbreak. Report disease incidents to public health authorities. Immunoglobulin (IG) recommended for protection of close contacts.

(continued)

TABLE 6   Common Communicable Illnesses (Continued)

Communicable Illness	Signs and Symptoms	Infectious Agent	Methods of Transmission	Incubation Period	Length of Communicability	Control Measures
Pinworms	Irritability, and itching of the rectal area. Common among young children. Some children have no symptoms.	Parasite; not contagious from animals.	Infectious eggs are transferred from person to person by contaminated hands (oral-fecal route). Indirectly spread by contaminated bedding, food, clothing, swimming pool.	Life cycle of the worm is 3–6 weeks; persons can also reinfect themselves.	2–8 weeks or as long as a source of infection remains present.	Infected children must be excluded from school until treated with medication; may return after initial dose. All infected and noninfected family members must be treated at one time. Frequent hand washing is essential; discourage nail biting or sucking of fingers. Daily baths and change of linen are necessary. Disinfect school toilet seats and sink handles at least once a day. Vacuum carpeted areas daily. Eggs are also destroyed when exposed to temperatures over 132°F. Education and good personal hygiene are vital to control.
Salmonellosis	Abdominal pain and cramping, sudden fever, severe diarrhea (may contain blood), nausea and vomiting lasts 5–7 days.	Bacteria	Fecal-oral transmission: via dirty hands. Also contaminated food (especially improperly cooked poultry, milk, eggs) water supplies, and infected animals.	12–36 hours	Throughout acute illness; may remain a carrier for months.	Attempt to identify source. Exclude children/adults with diarrhea; may return when symptoms end. Carriers should not handle or prepare food until stool cultures are negative. Practice good hand-washing and sanitizing procedures.

Reprinted with permission, *Health, Safety, and Nutrition for the Young Child*, Marotz, Cross, and Rush, 2005. Thomson Delmar Learning.

TABLE 7 Recommended Childhood and Adolescent Immunization Schedule—United States, 2003

Legend:
- range of recommended ages
- catch-up vaccination
- preadolescent assessment

Vaccine ▼ / Age ▶	Birth	1 mo	2 mos	4 mos	6 mos	12 mos	15 mos	18 mos	24 mos	4-6 yrs	11-12 yrs	13-18 yrs
Hepatitis B[1]	HepB #1 only if mother HBsAg (-)	HepB #2		HepB #3							HepB series	
Diphtheria, Tetanus, Pertussis[2]			DTaP	DTaP	DTaP			DTaP		DTaP	Td	Td
Haemophilus influenzae Type b[3]			Hib	Hib	Hib	Hib						
Inactivated Polio[4]			IPV	IPV	IPV	IPV				IPV		
Measles, Mumps, Rubella[4]						MMR #1				MMR #2	MMR #2	
Varicella[5]						Varicella				Varicella		
Pneumococcal[6]			PCV	PCV	PCV	PCV	PCV			PCV	PPV	
Hepatitis A[7]										Hepatitis A series		
Influenza[8]						Influenza (yearly)						

Vaccines below this line are for selected populations

This schedule indicates the recommended ages for routine administration of currently licensed childhood vaccines, as of December 1, 2002, for children through age 18 years. Any dose not given at the recommended age should be given at any subsequent visit when indicated and feasible. ▨ Indicates age groups that warrant special effort to administer those vaccines not previously given. Additional vaccines may be licensed and recommended during the year. Licensed combination vaccines may be used whenever any components of the combination are indicated and the vaccine's other components are not contraindicated. Providers should consult the manufacturers' package inserts for detailed recommendations.

1. Hepatitis B vaccine (HepB). All infants should receive the first dose of hepatitis B vaccine soon after birth and before hospital discharge; the first dose may also be given by age 2 months if the infant's mother is HBsAg-negative. Only monovalent HepB can be used for the birth dose. Monovalent or combination vaccine containing HepB may be used to complete the series. Four doses of vaccine may be administered when a birth dose is given. The second dose should be given at least 4 weeks after the first dose, except for combination vaccines which cannot be administered before age 6 weeks. The third dose should be given at least 16 weeks after the first dose and at least 8 weeks after the second dose. The last dose in the vaccination series (third or fourth dose) should not be administered before age 6 months.

Infants born to HBsAg-positive mothers should receive HepB and 0.5 mL Hepatitis B Immune Globulin (HBIG) within 12 hours of birth at separate sites. These infants should be tested for HBsAg and anti-HBs at 9–15 months of age.

Infants born to mothers whose HBsAg status is unknown should receive the first dose of the HepB series within 12 hours of birth. Maternal blood should be drawn as soon as possible to determine the mother's HBsAg status; if the HBsAg test is positive, the infant should receive HBIG as soon as possible (no later than age 1 week). The second dose is recommended at age 1–2 months. The last dose in the vaccination series should not be administered before age 6 months.

2. Diphtheria and tetanus toxoids and acellular pertussis vaccine (DTaP). The fourth dose of DTaP may be administered as early as age 12 months, provided 6 months have elapsed since the third dose and the child is unlikely to return at age 15–18 months. **Tetanus and diphtheria toxoids (Td)** is recommended at age 11–12 years if at least 5 years have elapsed since the last dose of tetanus and diphtheria toxoid-containing vaccine. Subsequent routine Td boosters are recommended every 10 years.

3. *Haemophilus influenzae* type b (Hib) conjugate vaccine. Three Hib conjugate vaccines are licensed for infant use. If PRP-OMP (PedvaxHIB® or ComVax® [Merck]) is administered at ages 2 and 4 months, a dose at age 6 months is not required. DTaP/Hib combination products should not be used for primary immunization in infants at ages 2, 4 or 6 months, but can be used as boosters following any Hib vaccine.

4. Measles, mumps, and rubella vaccine (MMR). The second dose of MMR is recommended routinely at age 4–6 years but may be administered during any visit, provided at least 4 weeks have elapsed since the first dose and that both doses are administered beginning at or after age 12 months. Those who have not previously received the second dose should complete the schedule by the 11–12 year old visit.

5. Varicella vaccine. Varicella vaccine is recommended at any visit or after age 12 months for susceptible children, i.e. those who lack a reliable history of chickenpox. Susceptible persons aged ≥13 years should receive two doses, given at least 4 weeks apart.

6. Pneumococcal vaccine. The heptavalent **pneumococcal conjugate vaccine (PCV)** is recommended for all children age 2–23 months. It is also recommended for certain children age 24–59 months. **Pneumococcal polysaccharide vaccine (PPV)** is recommended in addition to PCV for certain high-risk groups. See *MMWR* 2000;49(RR-9);1–38.

7. Hepatitis A vaccine. Hepatitis A vaccine is recommended for children and adolescents in selected states and regions, and for certain high-risk groups; consult your local public health authority. Children and adolescents in these states, regions, and high risk groups who have not been immunized against hepatitis A can begin the hepatitis A vaccination series during any visit. The two doses in the series should be administered at least 6 months apart. See *MMWR* 1999;48(RR-12);1–37.

8. Influenza vaccine. Influenza vaccine is recommended annually for children age ≥6 months with certain risk factors (including but not limited to asthma, cardiac disease, sickle cell disease, HIV, diabetes, and household members of persons in groups at high risk; see *MMWR* 2002;51(RR-3);1–31), and can be administered to all others wishing to obtain immunity. In addition, healthy children age 6–23 months are encouraged to receive influenza vaccine if feasible because children in this age group are at substantially increased risk for influenza-related hospitalizations. Children aged ≤12 years should receive vaccine in a dosage appropriate for their age (0.25 mL if age 6–35 months or 0.5 mL if aged ≥3 years). Children aged ≤8 years who are receiving influenza vaccine for the first time should receive two doses separated by at least 4 weeks.

For additional information about vaccines, including precautions and contraindications for immunization and vaccine shortages, please visit the National Immunization Program Website at www.cdc.gov/nip or call the National Immunization Information Hotline at 800-232-2522 (English) or 800-232-0233 (Spanish).

Approved by the Advisory Committee on Immunization Practices (www.cdc.gov/nip/acip), the American Academy of Pediatrics (www.aap.org), and the American Academy of Family Physicians (www.aafp.org).

Reprinted with permission, *Health, Safety, and Nutrition for the Young Child*, Marotz, Cross, and Rush, 2005. Thomson Delmar Learning.

TABLE 8   Guidelines for Administering Medication to Children

1. Be honest when giving young children medication! Do not use force or attempt to trick children into believing that medicines are candy. Instead, use the opportunity to help children understand the relationship between taking a medication and recovering from an illness or infection. Also, acknowledge the fact that the taste of medicine may be disagreeable or a treatment may be somewhat unpleasant; offer a small sip of juice or cracker to eliminate an unpleasant taste or read a favorite story as a reward for cooperating.

2. Designate one individual to accept medication from parents and administer it to children; this could be the director or the head teacher. This step helps minimize the opportunity for errors, such as omitting a dose or giving a dose twice.

3. When medication is accepted from a parent, it should be in the original container, labeled with the child's name, name of the drug, and directions for the exact amount and frequency the medication is to be given.

   Caution: NEVER give medicine from a container that has been prescribed for another individual.

4. Store all medicines in a locked cabinet. If it is necessary to refrigerate a medication, place it in a locked box and store on a top shelf in the refrigerator.

5. Be sure to wash your hands before and after administering medication.

6. Concentrate on what you are doing and do not talk with anyone until you are finished.

   a. Read the label on the bottle or container three times:
      - when removing it from the locked cabinet
      - before pouring it from the container
      - after pouring it from the container

   b. Administer medication on time and give *only* the amount prescribed.

   c. Be sure you have the correct child! If the child is old enough to talk, ask "What is your name?" and let the child state his/her name.

7. Record and maintain a permanent record of each dose of medicine that is administered. Include the:
   - date and time the medicine was given
   - name of the teacher administering the medication
   - dose of medication given
   - any unusual physical changes or behaviors observed after the medicine was administered

8. Inform parents of the dosage(s) and time medication was given, as well as any unusual reactions that may have occurred.

9. Adults should never take any medication in front of children.

Reprinted with permission, *Health, Safety, and Nutrition for the Young Child,* Marotz, Cross, and Rush, 2005. Thomson Delmar Learning.

Indicators of Visual Problems

Problems with children's eyesight can be recognized before major problems develop if teachers carefully observe early warning signs. The following list provides information on a few of the indicators of possible vision problems:

- Strains to see distant objects

- Poor eye-hand coordination

- Blurred and watery eyes

- Blinks often when trying to do close-up work

- Short attention span when doing tasks that require vision

- Tilts head to the side when trying to see something

- Appears clumsy and stumbles over things

- May cross eyes at times

- Frequent headaches

Be careful to avoid making preliminary conclusions about children's vision without looking at multiple sources of information. As with any type of health concern, the teacher's job is to carefully observe and document a supposed problem before making premature judgments. If a genuine pattern of complaints persists, it is important to make referrals to medical professionals.

Dental Concerns

Healthy diets, good oral hygiene, and early visits to the dentist prior to the age of two can keep children on the pathway to good dental health. Most of the trips to the dentist before the age of three are for preventive care and to educate the children about the importance of caring for their teeth. Temporary teeth serve four major purposes: chewing, holding spaces for the permanent teeth, shaping the jawbone, and helping in the development of speech (Marotz, 2005).

It is important for teachers to observe young children carefully for signs of dental problems. The following list gives some suggestions for observation:

- Make sure that the inside of the cheeks have an even color throughout.

- Make sure gums are not swollen or discolored.

- Make sure the same number of teeth are on both sides of the midpoint of the jaw.

- Make sure the teeth touch properly when the mouth is closed.

- Make sure there are no dark spots or pits on the teeth.

- Make sure there are no broken teeth.

- Make sure the teeth are clean without an offensive smell. (Aronson, 2002)

ABUSE AND NEGLECT

Although abuse and neglect can happen in any type of family or socioeconomic group, several situational stresses increase the risk. Observant teachers can often spot potential risk factors and get help for the families. Some of the situational stresses include isolation from others, domestic violence in the home, presence of a non-biologically related male, financial problems, single parenthood, substance abuse, and teen parents (Aronson, 2002). Table 9 can be used to assist teachers as they work with children and families who might have many situational risk factors.

TABLE 9   Observation List for Recognizing Abused and Neglected Children

- repeated or unexplained injuries, e.g., burns, fractures, bruises, bites, eye or head injuries
- frequently complains of pain
- wears clothing to hide injuries; may be inappropriate for weather conditions
- reports harsh treatment
- frequently late or absent; arrives too early or stays after dismissal from school
- unusually fearful of adults, especially parents
- appears malnourished or dehydrated
- avoids logical explanations for injuries
- withdrawn, anxious, or uncommunicative, or may be outspoken and disruptive
- lacks affection, both giving and seeking
- may be given inappropriate food, beverage, or drugs

Physical Abuse

- generally unhappy; seldom smiles or laughs
- aggressive and disruptive or unusually shy and withdrawn
- reacts without emotion to unpleasant statements and actions

(continued)

TABLE 9　Observation List for Recognizing Abused and Neglected Children (Continued)

- displays behaviors that are unusually adultlike or childlike
- delayed growth and/or emotional and intellectual development

Emotional Abuse

- underclothing torn, stained, or bloody
- complains of pain or itching in the genital area
- has venereal disease
- has difficulty getting along with other children, e.g., withdrawn, babylike, anxious
- rapid weight loss or gain
- sudden failure in school performance
- involved in delinquency, including prostitution, running away, alcoholism, or drug abuse
- fascination with body parts, talks about sexual activities

Sexual Abuse

- repeatedly arrives unclean; may have a bad odor from dirty clothing or hair
- is in need of medical or dental care; may have untreated injuries or illness
- frequently hungry; begs or steals food while at school
- dresses inappropriately for weather conditions; shoes and clothing often sized too small or too large
- is chronically tired; falls asleep at school, lacks the energy to play with other children
- has difficulty getting along with other children; spends much time alone

Physical Neglect

- poor academic performance
- appears apathetic, withdrawn and inattentive
- frequently absent or late to school
- uses any means to gain teacher's attention and approval
- seldom participates in extracurricular activities
- engages in delinquent behaviors, e.g., stealing, vandalism, sexual misconduct, abuse of drugs or alcohol

Reprinted with permission, *Health, Safety and Nutrition for the Young Child,* Marotz, Cross, and Rush, 2005. Thomson Delmar Learning.

SPECIAL ISSUES AFFECTING HEALTH

The inclusion of special needs children into classrooms has benefits for all the children in the program. Children with a wide variety of special needs, such as language delays, developmental delays, chronic illnesses, physical disabilities, and children at risk for emotional disorders, can benefit from inclusion in a quality early childhood classroom.

Program directors often fear that they will be asked to make modifications that are costly to their program. The goal of the Americans with Disabilities Act is that programs will make reasonable accommodations for individuals with disabilities so that integration into the program is made possible to the extent that it is feasible. Consideration is given to each individual's limitation. The principles of the ADA focus on three key words: individuality, reasonableness, and integration. Individuality refers to the unique limitations of the child. Reasonableness refers to the types of realistic modifications that might need to be made to the program. Integration refers to the involvement of the child with others in the classroom. Reasonable modifications to the program might include things like adding equipment to improve communication, making policy and procedural changes, and removing physical barriers, such as furniture and equipment that would prevent participation by the individual with disabilities. Programs are not asked to make changes that would put an undue burden on the program or fundamentally alter the nature of the program. Structural changes that will be very costly and difficult for the program are not required. Facilities built after January, 1993, however, must comply with ADA Accessibility Guidelines. If any new structural changes are made to buildings built before that time, the building must be brought up to meet the current ADA standards as well. Remember that the goal of inclusion is not to cause a threat to the individual with a disability or to anyone in the program. The goal of inclusion is that all children benefit from the diversity that is a part of our world.

PLANNING FOR HEALTH EDUCATION OPPORTUNITIES

- Additional Suggestions for Health Activities with Children
- Health Case Scenarios with Questions to Consider
- Current Trends in the Area of Health
- What Can I Do To Support the Healthy Growth of Children in My Care?
- Resources

ACTIVITY PLANS

Activity Plan #1: Protecting Skin and Eyes from Sun Damage

Concept: The sun can cause damage to skin and eyes if protection is not used properly.

Objectives:

- Children can describe why it is important to protect skin from sun damage.
- Children can describe why it is important to protect eyes from sun damage.
- Children can demonstrate selection of items needed for protection from the sun.

Materials List: Construction paper of different colors, flat items to lay on the construction paper, sunglasses, hats, sunscreen, pictures of people at the beach or outside in the sunshine, small bag, sunshine

Learning Activities:

A. Begin with a book about enjoying the outdoors in the sun. Ask open-ended questions about the book that will lead to a discussion of how the people in the pictures are dressed and what types of things they need to do to protect themselves from the sun.

B. After sharing the book, have several items used by people when they are in the sun. Be sure to include such items as sunglasses, hat, sunscreen, small folded umbrella, and so on. Have children take turns reaching in the bag and guessing what they are touching. Encourage them to use language skills as they give terms to describe the size and shape of the objects.

C. Lead children in a discussion of why the items from the bag are used when people are out in the sunshine.

D. Place a group of items or pictures of items on a table. Have children select the items that will be helpful to protect their skin and eyes from the sun. Be sure regular hand lotion and sunscreen is included so that children can learn the difference between the two types of products.

E. Place items on the construction paper and place them in a dry spot located in direct sunlight. Have the children go back and check them the next day to see the results. It is very effective to use different types of items, such as cheese cloth, paper, sunglasses lenses, clear glass, lotion, and so on.

Evaluation:

1. Were the children able to describe why protection from the sun's rays is important?

2. Were the children able to identify items needed for protection while in the sunshine?

Activity Plan # 2: Germs on the Grow

Concept: Germs that are not properly washed away will grow and can be passed on to others.

Objectives:

- Children will describe how proper hand washing can decrease the spread of germs.

- Children will explain the differences in growth of bacteria that result from poor hand washing.

Materials List: Canned biscuits, plastic bags, soap, water

Learning Activities:

A. After coming inside from playing outside, students will discuss things they have touched that might have germs. Discuss with the children the importance of washing hands to remove germs.

B. Review the proper techniques for hand washing with the children. Demonstrate and have them practice using a song or finger play to remind them of the technique. It is often suggested that children wash their hands for about the amount of time that it takes to sing the song, Happy Birthday.

C. Take the canned biscuits and have a few children press their unwashed hands into the biscuit to make a hand print. Have a few other children wash their hands thoroughly using the techniques discussed earlier. Place each of the biscuits in a labeled bag. Place the biscuits aside in a place where they can be easily observed.

D. Have the children make observations of the bacterial growth on the bread.

Evaluation:

1. Were the children able to describe the differences in the growth of bacteria and the reasons for those differences?

2. Were the children able to demonstrate the proper hand washing techniques?

Activity Plan # 3: Exercise Pays Off

Concept: Exercise benefits the body by increasing its strength and stamina

Objectives:

- Children will describe the ways in which exercise increases the strength of the body.

- Children will describe the ways in which exercise increases the ability of the body to do more work without getting tired.

- Children will identify enjoyable ways to add more exercise to their lives.

Materials List: Stopwatch or a watch with a second hand, pictures of people doing different types of activities (include physical and nonphysical activities), a place to move vigorously

Learning Activities:

A. Have children locate the spot in their neck where they can easily feel their pulse. Discuss the importance of the heart and how it pumps blood to all parts of the body. Ask them questions such as:

   1. What do you do if you want to get your muscles stronger?

   2. If your heart is a muscle, how can you make it stronger?

B. Have the children move vigorously around the room. Using music will help them start and stop the moving at the proper cues. After the vigorous movement, have them once again feel the pulse in their neck. They can also feel their heart beating in their chest. Ask them questions such as:

   1. Why is your heart beating faster now?

   2. Why do you think it needs to beat faster as you exercise?

   3. How do you think your heart gets stronger?

   Lead children to an understanding of the relationship between exercise that increases the heart rate and the strength of the heart muscle.

C. Have the children discuss what types of activities they do when they get home. Have them describe which types of activities will increase the strength of their bodies and their heart.

D. Place pictures of various types of activities out for the children to see. Have them select the pictures showing people doing healthy activities that make their bodies stronger.

Evaluation:

1. Were the children able to explain how exercise benefits the body?

2. Were the children able to identify healthy physical activities?

ADDITIONAL SUGGESTIONS FOR HEALTH ACTIVITIES WITH CHILDREN

- Let the children do a survey and an investigation on where germs might be hiding.

- Do flannelboard activities to help children understand some of the ways in which germs are transmitted (air, hands, contact surfaces, blood, food, saliva).

- Have children brainstorm about ways they can help cut down on the spread of germs in their own classroom.

- Prepare an activity to help children understand how glasses work to help the eyes see better.

- As a part of a body awareness unit, help the children learn to identify the parts of their body and how our body helps tell us when we are not keeping it healthy.

- Plan activities that help children discover what types of practices help keep teeth healthy.

- Help the children learn the roles of the various healthcare professionals who monitor their health.

- Use songs and finger plays to help the children understand proper hand washing techniques.

- Use a matching game where children have to select the appropriate types of clothing for the activity and weather in which they might participate.

- Read books about emotions and have children play games to help identify and understand various types of emotions.

- Plan activities designed to help children understand the proper procedures for brushing teeth and the correct way to brush.

For a listing of children's books that can be used to help children understand health concepts, please see the "Books for Children" section at the end of this book.

HEALTH CASE SCENARIOS WITH QUESTIONS TO CONSIDER

Health Case Scenario #1:

A parent hurriedly bring a child into the classroom and prepares to leave telling you that Johnny was feeling a little tired this morning, but he should be okay. She said to call her if you need her. As you look at the child, you see that his eyes look weak and his color is somewhat flushed. You touch the child's forehead, but do not notice any fever. During the morning, Johnny does not participate as he usually does. A couple of hours after the mother is gone, you notice that Johnny seems hot and feverish. You take his temperature and it registers at 101.5 degrees. When you call his mother, she tells you that she gave him Tylenol this morning before she brought him to school because she really needed to be at work this morning.

Questions to Consider

1. What standard procedures could have been put into place to prevent situations like this?

2. How would the use of regular daily morning health assessments be of help here?

3. What supports does this parent lack that might be helpful to avoid this situation?

4. How will you tactfully help the parent understand the importance of the health risks to her child and to others?

Health Case Scenario #2:

There is a five-year-old in your classroom who is quickly becoming obese. As he arrives each morning, he is finishing the pop tarts and soda that he had in the car on the way to school. He is becoming less able to participate in the running and playing activities that most of the children enjoy. Some of the children are beginning to leave him out of their games, and they laugh when he tries to run. You have already discovered that the child goes to his grandmother's home in the afternoon, where he watches television and munches on chips and more soda until his mother returns to pick him up. The usual dinner is composed of fast food take-outs because the mother is too tired to prepare a meal for the two of them in the evening.

Questions to Consider

1. What life-style challenges seem to complicate the issues of health for this young child?

2. What connections do you see between the physical condition of this child and other domains of development?

3. What types of cycles do you see developing with the lack of exercise and poor diet?

4. What types of things could you plan in your classroom to help this child?

5. How would you work with this mother, grandmother, and child to improve the health benefits for this child?

Health Case Scenario #3:

A teenage mom brings her four-year-old child into the classroom each day. The child is slightly overweight and tall for her age. The child's teeth are rotten on the top and bottom at the center of the front rows of teeth. When you ask the mother about this, she has no answer. One day you see the child arriving at school with the mother. As they get out of the car the child hands a baby bottle of juice to her mother. After further questioning, the mother admits that the child goes to sleep with the bottle and that she always has a bottle in the car so that she will be quiet.

Questions to Consider

1. What is the probable cause of the rotten areas in the front rows of teeth?

2. What type of information will you share with the mother concerning dental health?

3. What other types of information and additional supports might be helpful for this mother and child?

CURRENT TRENDS IN THE AREA OF HEALTH

■ There is a great decrease in the amount of exercise that America's youth gets today. Many programs have added fitness components for young children.

■ An increase in cases of domestic violence and child abuse means that teachers must be more observant for warning signs of problems.

■ More children are on medication for either depression or hyperactivity than in the past.

■ With the passage of No Child Left Behind, significant reform has been mandated to the K–12 educational system. This legislation also includes provisions to strengthen partnerships with Head Start, Even Start, and other Early Childhood programs.

■ There is an increased concern over the great stress in which many children and families live today. This stress is a great concern to teachers of young children because when children are stressed, they typically do not eat the right types of food and are more prone to accidents. This is a good example of how the components of health, safety, and nutrition are intricately woven together.

WHAT CAN I DO TO SUPPORT THE HEALTHY GROWTH OF CHILDREN IN MY CARE?

- Educate children and families about healthy practices.

- Become aware of health organization and resources to share with parents.

- Make learning good health practices a part of the routines in the classroom.

- Be a role model of healthy practices.

- Include health activities and books as a part of the curriculum.

- Post picture reminders of healthy practices in strategic places for the children.

- Be careful to understand and follow the health guidelines and regulations.

- Maintain accurate and up-to-date health records on the children.

- Be observant in an effort to identify possible health problems early.

- Make health referrals when appropriate.

RESOURCES

Resources for Health Education
American Association for Health Education
1900 Association Drive
Reston, VA 20191
Online: http://www.aahperd.org

American Dental Association
211 E. Chicago Avenue
Chicago, IL 60611
Online: http://www.ada.org

American Public Health Association
800 I Street, NW
Washington, DC 20001
Online: http://www.apha.org

American Red Cross
8111 Gatehouse Road
Falls Church, VA 22042
Online: http://www.redcross.org

Centers for Disease Control and Prevention
1600 Clifton Road
Atlanta, GA 30333
Online: http://www.cdc.gov

Early Childhood Education Linkage System (ECELS)
(Healthy Child Care America)
Online: http://www.paaap.org

Emergency Medical Services for Children National Resource Center
111Michigan Avenue, NW
Washington, DC 20010
Online: http://www.ems-c.org

La Leche League International
1400 N. Meacham Road
Schaumburg, IL 60173
Online: http://www.lalecheleague.org

National Association for Sick Child Daycare
1716 5th Avenue North
Birmingham, AL 35203
Online: http://www.nascd.com

National Black Child Development Institute
1101 15th Street, NW Suite 900
Washington, DC 20005
Online: http://www.nbcdi.org

National Center for Education in Maternal and Child Health
2000 15th Street, N, Suite 701
Arlington, VA 22201
Online: http://www.ncemch.org

National SIDS Resource Center
2070 Chain Bridge Road, Suite 450

Vienna, VA 22182
Online: http://www.sidscenter.org

Prevent Child Abuse America
200 S. Michigan Avenue, 17th Floor
Chicago, IL 60604
Online: http://www.preventchildabuse.org

Resources for Chronically Ill Children
American Diabetes Association
1701 N. Beauregard Street
Alexandria, VA 22311
Online: http://diabetes.org

American Heart Association
727 Greenville Avenue
Dallas, TX 75231
Online: http://www.americanheart.org

American Lung Association
61 Broadway, 6th Floor
New York, NY 10006
Online: http://www.lungusa.org

Asthma and Allergy Foundation of America
1233 20th Street, NW Suite 402
Washington, DC 20036
Online: http://www.aafa.org

Epilepsy Foundation of America
4351 Garden City Drive
Landover, MD 20785
Online: http://www.efa.org

Sickle Cell Disease Association of America, Inc.
200 Corporate Point, Suite 495
Culver City, CA
Online: http://www.sicklecelldisease.org

Resources for Children with Special Needs
American Academy of Pediatrics
141 Northwest Point Boulevard
Elk Grove Village, IL 60007-1098
Online: http://www.aap.org

American Foundation for the Blind
11 Penn Plaza, Suite 300
New York, NY 10001
Online: http://www.afb.org

American Speech-Language-Hearing Association
10801 Rockville Pike
Rockville, MD 20852
Online: http://www.asha.org

The ARC
1010 Wayne Avenue, Suite 650
Silver Spring, MD 20910
Online: http://www.thearc.org

Autism Society of America
7910 Woodmont Avenue, Suite 300
Bethesda, MD 20814
Online: http://www.autism-society.org

Child Care Law Center
4120 Marathon Street
Los Angeles, CA 94104
Online: http://www.childcarelaw.org

Council for Exceptional Children
1110 N. Glebe Road, Suite 300
Arlington, VA 22201
Online: http://www.cec.sped.org

Epilepsy Foundation of America
4351 Garden City Drive
Landover, MD 20785
Online: http://www.efa.org

Learning Disabilities Association of America
4156 Library Road
Pittsburg, PA 15234
Online: http://www.ldanatl.org

March of Dimes Birth Defects Foundation
1275 Mamaroneck Avenue
White Plains, NY 10605
Online: http://www.modimes.org

National Attention Deficit Disorder Association
1788 Second Street, Suite 200
Highland Park, IL 60035
Online: http://www.add.org

National Down Syndrome Society
666 Broadway, 8th Floor
New York, NY 10012
Online: http://www.ndss.org

National Information Center for Children and Youth with
Disabilities
P.O. Box 1492
Washington, DC 20013
Online: http://www.nichcy.org

National Mental Health Association
2001 N. Beauregard Street
12th Floor
Alexandria, VA 22311
Online: http://www.nmha.org

United Cerebral Palsy Association, Inc
1660 L Street, NW Suite 700
Washington, DC 20036
Online: http://www.ucpa.org

WEB HIGHLIGHTS

The Early Childhood Education Linkage System (ECELS) is associated with the Pennsylvania Chapter of the American Academy of
Pediatrics. It provides information about childhood diseases and
other health issues facing children and is an excellent reference on
good practices.

   http://www.paaap.org

The Global Healthy Childcare site has printable charts related to
health and safety. It also has provides information relating to guidelines for health and safety that should be observed in the classroom.

   http://globalhealthychildcare.org

ASSESSMENT AND OBSERVATION TOOLS FOR SAFETY

IMPORTANT CONSIDERATIONS IN PLANNING FOR SAFE PROGRAMS

Safety exemplifies safe and secure. Clearly, the nature of a child's environment plays a critical role in the child's overall development. Emphasis on safety must be a critical component of every program that involves children.

To ensure that programs are safe, provide environments of high quality by emphasizing the following:

- Safety management

- Quality supervision

- Developmentally appropriate practices indoors and outdoors

- Compliance with local and state licensing requirements

- Freedom from harmful items, materials, and supplies

- The reduction and prevention of accidents

- Management of injuries, unintentional accidents, and illness

- The awareness of abuse and neglect identification

- The knowledge of reporting abuse and neglect laws as well as victim support

- Planning and implementing safety concept lessons for children

- Planning and implementing parent involvement opportunities for all families

DEVELOPMENTAL CHARACTERISTICS AND INJURY PREVENTION

Fully understanding developmental characteristics is essential to providing a safe and secure environment for all children. This awareness and understanding will help prevent injuries. Refer to the following list for some developmental considerations for very young children:

Age: 0–4 Months
Developmental Characteristics for Safety: Eats, sleeps, cries, rolls off of flat surfaces, wiggles

Hazards: burns, falls, choking, sharp objects, suffocation

Age: 4–12 Months
Developmental Characteristics for Safety: Grasps and moves about, puts objects into mouth

Hazards: Play areas, toys, small objects, poisoning, burns, falls

Age: 1–2 Years
Developmental Characteristics for Safety: Investigates, opens doors, takes things apart, climbs up on things

Hazards: Windows, gates, water, poisons, burns, play areas

Many varieties of toys and play equipment are used to enhance a child's learning experiences. Safety must be emphasized when selecting toys and play equipment for use with children of all ages. The following guidelines can be helpful when selecting safe toys and equipment for play (Marotz, 2002):

- Consider the child's age and interests as well as developmental characteristics.

- Select washable items made of flame-retardant materials.

- Select durable toys and items of high quality.

- Avoid items with sharp corners or strings longer than 12 inches.

- Avoid toys and materials with small pieces.

- Select toys and equipment that are appropriate for the amount of space for play and storage.

- Avoid toys with electrical parts.

- Choose toys and materials that can be used with minimal adult supervision.

PLAY MATERIALS FOR CHILDREN

Children construct their own understanding of the world around them as they interact with appropriate materials and with other people. Teachers play an important role in providing choices of good-quality playthings that match children's developmental abilities and interests. When budgets are limited, teachers must be able to select toys and materials that provide optimum learning opportunities. Creative teachers learn how to "scrounge" for toys and how to make playthings out of recycled materials.

CRITERIA FOR SELECTING PLAY EQUIPMENT FOR YOUNG CHILDREN

A young child's playthings should be as free of detail as possible.

- Too much detail hampers a child's freedom to express himself or herself.

- "Unstructured" toys, which allow the imagination free rein, include blocks, construction sets, clay, sand, and paints.

A good plaything should stimulate children to do things for themselves.

- Equipment that makes the child a spectator may entertain but has little or no play value.

- Play equipment should encourage children to explore and create or offer dramatic play potential.

Young children need large, easily manipulated playthings.

- Toys too small can be frustrating because the child's undeveloped muscular coordination cannot handle smaller forms and shapes.

- A child's muscles develop through play, so equipment should allow for climbing and balancing.

The material of which a plaything is constructed has an important role in the play of the young child.

- Warmth and pleasurable touch are significant (wood and cloth are the most satisfactory materials).

- The plaything's durability is of utmost importance.

- Play materials must be sturdy; axles and wheels must be able to support a child's weight.

- Children hate to see their toys break.

- Some materials break readily, which makes them expensive.

The toy must "work."

- Be sure parts move correctly.

- Make sure maintenance will be easy.

A plaything's construction should be simple enough for a child to comprehend.

- This strengthens the child's understanding and experience of the world.

- Mechanics should be visible and easily grasped; small children will take them apart to see how they tick.

A plaything should encourage cooperative play.

- Provide an environment that stimulates children to work and play together.

The total usefulness of the plaything must be considered in comparing price.

- Will it last several children through several stages of their playing lives?

The lists that follow suggest the materials that are priorities for children at particular levels of development.

FOR YOUNG INFANTS BIRTH THROUGH SIX MONTHS

- unbreakable mirrors that can be attached low on walls or near changing tables and cribs
- stuffed, washable toys or rag dolls, with stitched faces and eyes
- mobiles and visuals hung out of reach
- grasping toys: simple rattles, squeeze toys, keys on ring, clutch or texture balls
- hanging toys for batting
- wrist or ankle bells

FOR OLDER, MOBILE INFANTS 7 THROUGH 12 MONTHS

- soft rubber animals for grasping
- simple one-piece vehicles 6–8 inches, with large wheels
- grasping toys for skill development: toys on suction cups, stacking rings, nesting cups, squeeze toys, plastic pop beads, bean bags, busy boxes
- containers and objects to fill and dump
- small cloth, plastic, and board books
- soft cloth or foam blocks for stacking
- simple floating objects for water play
- balls of all kinds, including some with special effects
- low, soft climbing platforms
- large unbreakable mirrors
- infant swings for outdoors
- recorded music and songs

FOR TODDLERS ONE TO THREE YEARS

For Fine Motor Skills:

- nesting materials
- sand and water play toys: funnels, colanders, small sand tools
- simple activity boxes, with doors, lids, switches, more complex after about 18 months: turning knob or key

- pegboards with large pegs

- four- or five-piece stacking materials

- pop beads and stringing beads

- simple three- to five-piece puzzles with knobs, familiar shapes

- simple matching materials

- books, including tactile books, cloth, plastic, and board picture books

For Gross Motor Skills:

- push and pull toys

- simple doll carriages and wagons

- stable riding toys with four wheels and no pedals

- balls of all sizes

- tunnels for crawling through

- tumbling mats and low climbing platforms

For Pretend Play:

- small wood or plastic people and animal figures

- small cars and trucks

- dolls

- plastic dishes and pots and pans

- doll beds

- hats

- simple dress-ups

- telephones

- scarves and fabrics

For Sensory Play:

- recorded music and player

- play dough

- fingerpaint

- large nontoxic crayons
- sturdy paper
- simple musical instruments

FOR CHILDREN THREE THROUGH FIVE

For Gross Motor Play:

- small wagons and wheelbarrows
- replications of adult tools for pushing and pretend play, such as lawn mower, shopping cart
- scooters
- tricycles and other vehicles with steering ability
- riding toys for more than one child
- balls of all sizes, especially 10-inch and 12-inch balls for kicking and throwing
- hollow plastic bat and lightweight ball
- jump rope
- stationary outdoor climbing equipment
- slides and ladders
- outdoor building materials, tires, and other loose parts

Exploration and Mastery Play Materials:

- sand and water play: measures, funnels, tubes, sand tools
- construction materials: unit blocks, large hollow blocks
- Lego-type plastic interlocking blocks
- puzzles, including fit-in puzzles and large, simple jigsaw puzzles, with varying numbers of pieces, according to children's age
- pattern-making materials: beads for stringing, pegboards, mosaic boards, feltboards, color cubes
- dressing, lacing, and stringing: sewing cards and dressing frames
- collections of small plastic objects for matching, sorting, and ordering by color, shape, size, or other category concepts

- simple, concrete number materials for counting and matching to numerals

- measuring materials: scales, measuring cups for liquids

- science materials: magnifying glass, color paddles, objects from the natural world, including pets

- beginning computer programs

- games: dominoes; lotto games; bingo by color, number, or picture; first board games that use concepts such as color or counting; memory

- books of all kinds: picture books, realistic stories, alphabet picture books, poetry, information books

- writing center materials: clipboards, colored pencils, old calendars, envelopes, notepads, stationery, rubber stamps and ink pads, rulers, magnetic letters, stencil shapes, stickers, file cards, and office materials

For Pretend Play:

- dolls of various ethnic and gender appearance, with clothes and other accessories and furniture

- housekeeping equipment

- variety of dress-ups, including those related to various roles and themes

- transportation toys

- hand puppets

- animal and human figures for play scenes

- full-length, unbreakable mirror

For Creative Play:

- art and craft materials: crayons, markers, easel, paintbrushes, paint and fingerpaint, varieties of paper, chalkboard and chalk, safety scissors, glue, collage materials, clay and play dough, and tools to use with them

- workbench with hammer, saw, and nails

- musical instruments

- recorded music for singing, movement and dancing, listening, and for using with rhythm instruments

FOR CHILDREN SIX THROUGH EIGHT YEARS

For Gross Motor Play:

- balls and sports equipment for beginning team play, such as soccer, baseball
- complex climbing structures: ropes, ladders, rings, hanging bars
- materials for target practice
- mats for acrobatics
- bicycles and scooters

For Exploration and Mastery Play:

- construction materials for large constructions and for creating models, including metal parts and nuts and bolts
- puzzles: 100-piece jigsaw puzzles, three-dimensional puzzles such as Rubik's cubes
- craft materials for braiding, weaving, knitting, leather craft, jewelry making, sewing
- pattern-making materials: mosaic tiles, geometric puzzles
- games: word games, simple card games, reading and spelling games, number and counting games, beginning strategy games such as checkers
- materials for specific learning: printing materials, math manipulatives, measuring materials, science materials, and computer programs for language arts, number and concept development, and for problem-solving activities
- books at a variety of levels for beginning readers

For Creative Activities:

- variety of markers, colored pencils, chalks, paintbrushes and paints, art papers for tracing and drawing
- clay and tools, including pottery wheel
- workbench with wood and variety of tools
- real instruments such as guitars and recorders
- music for singing and movement
- audiovisual materials for independent use

Some ideas adapted from *The Right Stuff for Children Birth to 8: Selecting Play Materials to Support Development.* M. Bronson. Washington, D.C.: NAEYC, 1995.

HAZARDOUS ART MATERIALS

Art time can be a very exciting and beneficial part of a child's learning experiences. Safety must also be stressed during this time of learning. Teachers must insure that all materials used by children are safe. Items such as dry powders, aerosol sprays, solvents, permanent markers, and items containing minerals and fibers should be avoided. Appropriate items include liquid tempera paints, nontoxic markers, water-based glues and paints, and natural vegetable dyes.

COMMON POISONOUS VEGETATION

Children are naturally curious about many things, which can lead to serious injuries and even death. An area of specific concern is poisonous vegetation.

Table 10 outlines some common poisonous vegetation that those working with or caring for children should know for prevention purposes.

TABLE 10   Some Common Poisonous Vegetation

Bittersweet berries	Causes a burning sensation in the mouth. Nausea, vomiting, dizziness, and convulsions.
Buttercup, all parts	Irritating to the digestive tract. Causes nausea and vomiting.
Castor bean beanlike pod	Extremely toxic. May be fatal to both children and adults.
Daffodil, hyacinth, narcissus, jonquil, iris roots, underground bulbs	Nausea, vomiting, and diarrhea. Can be fatal.
Dieffenbachia leaves	Causes immediate burning and swelling around mouth.
English Ivy leaves and berries	Ingestion results in extreme burning sensation.
Holly berries	Results in cramping, nausea, vomiting, and diarrhea.
Lily-of-the-Valley leaves and flowers	Nausea, vomiting, dizziness, and mental confusion.
Mistletoe berries	Extremely toxic. Diarrhea and irregular pulse.
Oleander flowers and sap	Highly toxic; can be fatal. Causes nausea, vomiting, diarrhea, and heart irregularities.
Philodendron leaves	Ingestion causes intense irritation and swelling of the lips and mouth.

(*continued*)

TABLE 10   Some Common Poisonous Vegetation (Continued)

Rhubarb, raw leaves	Can cause convulsions, coma, and rapid death.
Sweet pea, all parts, especially seeds	Shallow respirations, possible convulsions, paralysis, and slow pulse.
Black Locust tree bark, leaves, pods, and seeds	Causes nausea and weakness, especially in children.
Cherry tree leaves and twigs	Can be fatal. Causes shortness of breath, general weakness, and restlessness.
Golden chain tree beanlike seed pods	Can cause convulsions and coma.
Oak tree acorns and leaves	Eating large quantities may cause poisoning. Gradually causes kidney failure.
Rhododendron, all parts	Causes vomiting, convulsions, and paralysis.
Wisteria seed pods	Causes severe diarrhea and collapse.
Yew berries and foliage	Foliage is very poisonous and can be fatal. Causes nausea, diarrhea, and difficult breathing.

HEALTH AND SAFETY CHECKLIST—NAEYC

Checklists are necessary tools that guide our effectiveness in specific areas of performance and development. The National Association for the Education of Young Children has produced a *Healthy Young Children* manual that contains a comprehensive checklist for health and safety. Refer to the resource section for information on this book.

PLAYGROUND SAFETY RULES

Playground safety rules must always be followed to prevent accidents and to ensure that children benefit fully from their time interacting on the playground. Teachers and caregivers must understand the following:

- The playground is an extension of the indoor environment and another avenue of learning.

- Supervision is critical to safety.

- When children are waiting to use the playground equipment, they must stand back a safe distant to avoid being hit by those actively involved in play.

- Children must avoid using play equipment inappropriately.

Playground guidelines differ by state, so teachers must know and understand the guidelines specific to their state. NAEYC's *Healthy Programs for Young Children* book includes some general guidelines for consideration.

BE AWARE OF WHAT'S IN YOUR FIRST AID KIT

Make a monthly inspection of your first aid kit to note needed changes. The following items should be included:

- At least two pairs of latex gloves (use nonlatex if allergic reactions occur with the use of latex)

- Sterile dressings to stop bleeding

- Cleansing materials and supplies to prevent infections, such as antibiotic soap and water, antiseptics, burn ointment, a variety of adhesive bandages

- Safety pins

- Scissors and tweezers

- Materials to use as a splint

- Eye dressing and eye wash solution

- Cold pack

- Cell phone or coins for a pay telephone

- Emergency medical prescription information for children in your care

- Important telephone numbers:

  - Poison Control Center

  - Local Fire and Rescue Agencies

Be sure to have a current American Academy of Pediatrics Standard First Aid Chart to reference.

In addition to preparing for an emergency by having materials and supplies, parents and teachers must know how to effectively respond in the event of an emergency. To be sure that you are administering the correct form of treatment, refer to Table 11 which will assist you in assessing the emergency.

TABLE 11 The ABCs for Assessing Emergencies

A—Airway Make sure the air passageway is open and clear. Roll the infant or child onto his/her back. Tilt the head back by placing your hand on the child's forehead and gently push downward (unless back or neck injuries are suspected). At the same time, place the fingers of your other hand under the child's chin and lift it upward.

B—Breathing Watch for the child's chest to move up and down. Feel and listen for air to escape from the lungs with your ear.

C—Circulation Note the child's skin color (especially around the lips and nailbeds), and if the child is coughing or moving.

Reprinted with permission, *Health, Safety, and Nutrition for the Young Child*, Marotz, Cross, and Rush, 2005. Thomson Delmar Learning.

SPECIAL PRECAUTIONARY PROCEDURES

Absence of Breathing

Breathing emergencies accompany many life-threatening conditions, such as asthma, drowning, electrical shock, convulsions, poisoning, severe injuries, suffocating, choking, and Sudden Infant Death Syndrome (SIDS). Adults who work with young children should complete certified training in basic first aid and cardiopulmonary resuscitation (CPR). This training is available from most chapters of the American Red Cross and the American Heart Association or from a local ambulance service, rescue squad, fire department, high school, or community parks and recreation department.

It is important to remain calm and perform emergency life-saving procedures quickly and with confidence. Have someone call for an ambulance or emergency medical assistance while you begin mouth-to-mouth breathing. The procedure for mouth-to-mouth breathing follows and is also illustrated in Figure 2.

1. Gently shake the child or infant to determine if conscious or asleep. Call out the child's name in a loud voice. If there is no response, quickly assess the child's condition and immediately begin emergency breathing procedures.

2. Position the infant or child on his/her back on a hard surface. Using extreme care, roll an injured child as a unit, keeping the spine straight.

3. Remove any vomitus, excess mucus, or foreign objects (only if they can be seen) by quickly sweeping a finger around the inside of the child's mouth.

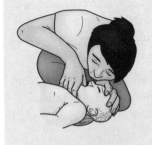

If vomitus or foreign objects are visible, use the tongue-jaw lift to open the mouth. Then use a finger to quickly check for the object. Remove if visible.

Position child on his/her back. Gently tilt the head up and back by placing one hand on child's forehead and fingers of the other hand under the jawbone. Lift upward (head tilt/chin lift). **Look** for the chest to rise/fall. **Listen** for breathing. **Feel** for breath on your cheek.

For an infant, place your mouth over the infant's nose and mouth creating a tight seal. Slowly and gently, give two small puffs of air (1–1$^1/_2$ seconds), pausing between breaths. Check (look/listen) for breathing at the rate of one breath every three seconds. If air does not go in, reposition and try to breathe again.

For a child one to eight years, place your mouth over the child's mouth forming a tight seal. Gently pinch the child's nostrils closed. Quickly give two small breaths of air (1–1$^1/_2$ seconds per breath). Continue breathing for the child at a rate of one breath every three seconds. If air does not go in, reposition and try to breathe again.

Lift your head and turn it to the side after each breath. This allows time for air to escape from the child's lungs and also gives you time to take a breath and to observe if the child is breathing.

Figure 2

4. To open the airway, gently tilt the child's head up and back by placing one hand on the forehead and *the fingers (not thumb)* of the other hand under the chin; push downward on the forehead and lift the chin upward.

   Caution: Do not tip the head back too far. Tipping the head too far can cause obstruction of the airway in an infant or small child. Keep your fingers on the jawbone, not on the tissue under the chin.

5. Listen carefully for 5–10 seconds for any spontaneous breathing by placing your ear next to the child's nose and mouth; also watch for a rise and fall of the chest and abdomen.

6. **For an infant,** place your mouth over the infant's nose and mouth to create a tight seal. Gently give two small puffs of air (1–1½ seconds per breath with a short pause in between) into the infant's nose and mouth.

   Caution: Too much air forced into an infant's lungs may cause the stomach to fill with air (may cause vomiting and increased risk of aspiration). Always remember to use small, gentle puffs of air from your cheeks.

7. **For the child one to eight years old,** gently pinch the nostrils closed, place your open mouth over the child's open mouth forming a tight seal. Give two small breaths (1–1½ seconds per breath) of air in quick succession, pausing between breaths.

8. Observe the child's chest and abdomen for movement (rising and falling) to be sure air is entering the lungs.

9. Continue breathing at the rate of one breath every 3 seconds for infants and children one to eight years; or, one breath every 5 seconds for children eight years and older.

10. Pull your mouth away and turn it to the side after giving each breath. This allows time for air to escape from the child's lungs and also gives you time to take a breath and see if the child is breathing on his or her own.

11. DO NOT GIVE UP! Continue breathing procedures until the child breathes alone or emergency medical assistance arrives. Failure to continue mouth-to-mouth breathing can lead to cardiac arrest in children.

If the entry of air seems blocked or the chest does not rise while administering mouth-to-mouth breathing, check for foreign objects in the mouth and airway and remove only if they are visible (refer to item number 4 on page 76). Continue mouth-to-mouth breathing until the child breathes alone or medical help arrives. If the child resumes breathing, keep him or her lying down and roll (as a unit) onto one side; this is called the recovery position. Maintain body temperature by covering with a light blanket. Closely observe the child's breathing until medical help arrives.

Choking

Different emergency techniques are used to treat infants, toddlers, and older children who are choking (American Heart Association, 2001). Regardless of the child's age, attempt to remove the object only if it can be clearly seen. Extreme care must be taken not to push the object further back into the airway. If the object cannot be removed easily, and the infant **IS CONSCIOUS**, quickly do the following:

- Have someone summon emergency medical assistance.

- Position the infant face down over the length of your arm, with the child's head lower than his or her chest and the head and neck supported in your hand (Figure 3). The infant can also be placed in your lap with its head lower than its chest.

- Use the heel of your hand to give five quick back blows between the infant's shoulder blades.

  Caution: Do not use excessive force as this could injure the infant.

- Support and turn the infant over, face up, with the head held lower than the chest.

- Give five chest thrusts, using the hand not supporting the infant's head. Place two fingers over the breastbone and approximately the width of one finger below the infant's nipples (Figure 4). Rapidly compress the infant's chest approximately ½–1 inch (1.3–2.5 cm); release pressure between thrusts, allowing the chest to return to its normal position.

- Look inside the child's mouth for the foreign body. If clearly visible and reachable, remove it.

- Repeat the steps alternating five back blows, five chest thrusts until the object is dislodged or the infant loses consciousness.

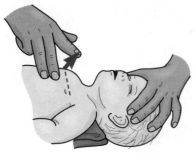

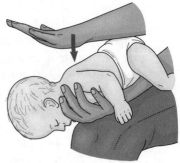

Figure 3   **Figure 4**

If the infant **LOSES CONSCIOUSNESS AND IS NOT BREATHING:**

- Have someone call for an ambulance or emergency medical assistance if this has not already been done.

- Place the infant on his or her back. Perform jaw lift. Look inside the child's mouth for the foreign body. If clearly visible and reachable, remove it.

- Begin lifesaving breathing procedures. Open the airway using head tilt/chin lift.

- Give the infant two small breaths of air, 1–1½ seconds per breath. Watch for the chest to rise and fall.

- If the infant's lungs inflate, continue breathing assistance, giving one breath every 3 seconds. If the lungs cannot be inflated, give one breath of air, five back blows, five chest thrusts, check in mouth for the object, reposition the airway, and give one breath of air. Repeat these steps until help arrives or the object is dislodged: **open airway, breath, five back blows, five chest thrusts, reposition the airway, breath.**

To give emergency aid to the child one to eight years who is choking, first attempt to remove the object from the blocked airway only if it is clearly visible and reachable. Use care not to push the object further back into the throat. If the object cannot be dislodged and the child **IS CONSCIOUS,** quickly do the following:

- Summon emergency medical assistance.

- Stand or kneel behind the child with your arms around the child's waist (Figure 5).

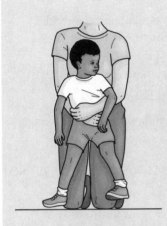

Stand or kneel behind the child with your arms around the child's waist.

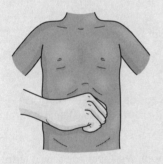

Make a fist with one hand. Place the fisted hand against the child's abdomen below the tip of the rib cage, slightly above the navel.

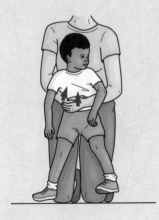

Grasp the fisted hand with your other hand. Press your fists into the child's abdomen with a quick upward thrust.

Figure 5

- Make a fist with one hand, thumbs tucked in.

- Place the fisted hand (thumb side) against the child's abdomen, midway between the base of the rib cage (xiphoid process) and the navel.

- Press your fisted hand into the child's abdomen with a quick, inward and upward thrust.

- Continue repeating abdominal thrusts until the object is dislodged or the child becomes unconscious.

If the child **LOSES CONSCIOUSNESS AND IS NOT BREATHING:**

- Immediately summon emergency medical assistance.

- Assess the ABCs first unless the victim is known to be choking.

- Place the child flat on the floor (on back, face up).

- Straddle the child's hips and kneel at the foot of a small child (Figure 6).

- Perform the jaw lift and look inside the child's mouth; carefully remove any object that is clearly visible and reachable.

- Begin lifesaving breathing procedures. Open the airway using head tilt/jaw lift technique. Give two small breaths of air, 1–1½ seconds each. Stop if the child begins breathing.

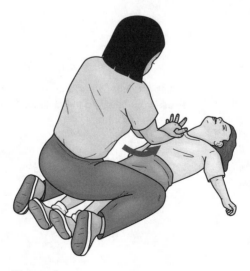

Figure 6

- If the child does not begin to breathe, place the heel of one hand on the child's abdomen, slightly above the navel and well below the base of the breastbone. Position the other hand on top of the first hand.

- Press hands into the child's abdomen with a quick upward thrust. Always keep hands positioned in the middle of the abdomen to avoid injuring nearby organs.

- Repeat abdominal thrusts five times. Repeat the sequence: **perform head tilt/chin lift technique, visually inspect the mouth for the object, attempt mouth-to-mouth breathing, give five abdominal thrusts and repeat the sequence. Do not give up!**

  Continue this sequence until the object is dislodged and you can get air in and out of the child's lungs or emergency medical help arrives.

- If the child begins to breathe on his own, stop mouth-to-mouth breathing, and continue to observe closely until medical help arrives. Roll the child (as a unit) onto his or her side (recovery position).

  After the object is dislodged and breathing is restored, always be sure the child receives medical attention.

Control Bleeding

Injuries or situations that involve the loss of blood are especially critical and require correcthandling. Thus, knowing how to control and stop the bleeding is vital. Figure 7 provides detailed information on the pressure points to use to control bleeding.

Child Safety Seats

Child safety seat laws can differ from state to state. However, nationally, most child restraint laws cover babies and children up to 4 years old or 40 pounds.

Refer to the National Highway and Transportation Safety Administration guide for child safety seat use:

- Rear-facing infant—Birth to 1 year and at least 20–22 lb

- Forward-facing—Over 1 year and over 20–40 lb

- Belt positioning booster—Over 40 lb. Ages 4–8, unless 4'9

Child Passenger Safety National Highway and Transportation Safety Administration. Retrieved 30 May 2005 http://www.nhtsa.dot.gov/nhtsa/whatis/regions/Region070/07cps.html.

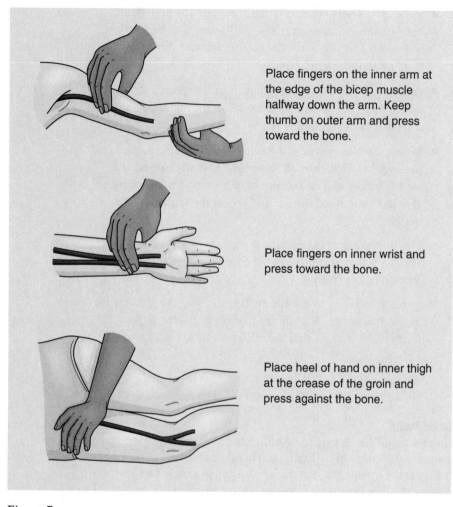

Place fingers on the inner arm at the edge of the bicep muscle halfway down the arm. Keep thumb on outer arm and press toward the bone.

Place fingers on inner wrist and press toward the bone.

Place heel of hand on inner thigh at the crease of the groin and press against the bone.

Figure 7
Reprinted with permission, *Health, Safety and Nutrition for the Young Child,* Marotz, Cross and Rush. 2005. Delmar Thomson Learning.

Hand Washing Is ALWAYS Helpful!

Hand washing is the first and most important step in the prevention of illness and the further spread of harmful disease and germs. Regardless of the role you fulfill with children, the washing of hands must be at the foundation if safety is a desired outcome.

Always remember and apply these preventive steps:

- Everyone entering the center, school, class, or learning environment should wash their hands.

Special emphasis must be placed on hand washing prior to and/or directly after the following:

- Handling and eating food

- Handling uncooked food (especially raw meat)

- Feeding a child

- Giving medication

- Using sand

- Playing in sand or water

- Changing diapers and clothing

- Removing or handling trash

- Using the toilet or assist a child during toileting

- Handling of any body fluids

- Handling of animals

Remember to encourage the children to wash their hands effectively and correctly.

Water Safety

Be aware that water can and does present many safety hazards and concerns. The potential for drowning and the transmission of illnesses are all possible dangers of time spent in bodies of water. This presents special concern for teachers. As with all child-centered activities, supervision is an absolute must at all times.

Water Play Safety Checklist:

☐ Can I see all children at all times?

☐ Are the water toys appropriate and located where children can easily access them?

☐ Is the water table stable to prevent slips and falls?

☐ Is the table located in an area to prevent slips and falls?

- Additional Suggestions for Safety Activities with Children
- Case Scenarios with Questions to Consider
- Current Trends in the Area of Safety
- What Can I Do to Support the Safety of Children in My Care?
- Resources

ACTIVITY PLANS

Activity Plan #1: I Can Be Safe Too!

Concept: Children can help to make the classroom safe by playing an active role.

Objectives:

- When presented with choices, children will be able to identify at least two ways the classroom is not a safe environment.

- Children will describe two ways to correct the concern to insure that the classroom environment is safe.

Materials List: Select poster board or a bulletin board to display a classroom setting, a playground, or any indoor or outdoor environment that children can use as a learning environment. Select materials such as foam, wallpaper, cloth material, construction paper, paper cups, or any safe materials or supplies to make environment items that will depend on which environment you decide to make. Velcro tape or any safe and appropriate adhesive material should be used to make the removable items readily reusable.

Learning Activities:

A. You will construct the environment background and items to be used in the selected environment. Your students will enjoy helping with this part of the assignment.

B. After all necessary furnishings and equipment are supplied. Add additional materials or items that do not belong to make the environment unsafe. For example, if you chose to use an outdoor environment, the playground, in addition to having sliding boards, climbers, and so on, add items such as trash and/or broken glass. These items will be used as materials to demonstrate how the environment is unsafe. The inappropriate items must be made out of safe materials because you will Velcro them to the board.

C. Read and discuss with the children what defines a safe and appropriate environment. Build motivation by asking questions such as, "Why is safety important?" "What could happen if our classroom is not safe?" Be sure to review previous taught lesson concepts and connect this to the current learning activity. Use visual and other materials to help them build understanding of what is safe and unsafe. Suggested books to read:

   Reasoner, C. (2003). *Bee Safe (The Bee Attitudes)*. Los Angeles: Price Stern Sloan Publishers.

   Schwartz, L. (1995). *The Safety Book for Active Kids: Teaching Your Child How to Avoid Everyday Dangers*. Santa Barbara, CA: Learning Works.

D. Discuss the environment display. Ask the children to share with you what is safe about the given environment. Allow the children to come and remove the items that make the environment unsafe.

E. Outline ways the children can correct safety concerns. Next, the children will describe two ways to correct the safety hazards they identified to insure that the classroom environment is safe.

F. Depending on the age group of your students, you could extend the activity by allowing them to identify other items in other environments that are not safe.

G. Conclude by reviewing the lesson objectives and by discussing why having safe environments are so important.

Evaluation:

1. Can the children identify at least two ways the classroom is not a safe environment by removing the inappropriate items for the displayed classroom or outdoor setting?

2. Can the children describe two ways to correct the concern to insure that the classroom environment is safe?

Activity Plan #2: Poisonous?—Do You Know!

Concept: Children can be active participants in making safe choices.

Objectives:

- Children will develop an awareness of the difference between safe and poisonous substances by asking an adult before they consume food or drinks.

- Children will follow precautionary steps to identify unsafe materials.

Materials List: Construction paper, drawing materials and supplies (to demonstrate the difference between safe liquids and foods and unsafe liquids and foods), resource book, and materials

Learning Activities:

A. Gather supplies to demonstrate the difference between safe liquids and foods and unsafe liquids and foods and other needed supplies.

B. Read about and discuss with the children what the word *poisonous* means. Build motivation by asking questions such as, "Why is understanding this so important?" "What could happen if you are around something poisonous?" Be sure to review previously taught lesson concepts and connect this to the learning activity. Use visual and other materials to help them build understanding of what is meant by poisonous. Suggested books to read:

O'Brien-Palmer, M. (1999). *Healthy Me: Fun Ways to Develop Good Health and Safety Habits: Activities for Children 5–8.* Chicago: Chicago Review Press.

C. Show the children how things we eat or drink can look like things we shouldn't eat or drink. Provide examples for the children to see.

D. Outline key ways children will be able to tell the difference between safe and unsafe materials. For example, point out that the most important first step is to ask an adult before eating or drinking anything. Reinforce the need for children to notice safety lids.

E. Conclude by reviewing the lesson objectives and by discussing why understanding what poisonous means and why this knowledge is so important. Check for understanding of what to do if an accident or ingestion of a poisonous substance occurs with them or another individual.

Evaluation:

1. Are children able to identify the difference between safe and poisonous substance?

2. Can the children follow precautionary steps to identify unsafe materials?

Activity Plan #3: Unfriendly Touches

Concept: Children should be taught the difference between appropriate and inappropriate touches.

Objective:

- Children will be able to distinguish the difference between appropriate and inappropriate touches.

Materials List: Poster board, construction paper, chart paper, drawing materials and supplies, resource book and materials, and premade hand cut-outs or hand cut-outs you made yourself.

Learning Activities:

A. Using selected materials, make two paper figures of a child, one female and the other male. Paste, post, or tape the paper figure to a poster board to display.

B. Read about and discuss with the children what is meant by appropriate or inappropriate touches. Build motivation by asking questions such as, "Why do we touch each other" "Can you list some happy touches, such as hugs and pats on the back?" "Can you list some unhappy touches, such as hitting and pushing?" Write down responses on chart paper to the previous questions.

C. Introduce the concept of appropriate and inappropriate touches. Discuss with the children how they will know the difference by providing age appropriate examples. Read the stories to reiterate the importance of informing adults when children are hurt or touched inappropriately. Suggested books:

Girard, L. (1987). *My Body Is Private*. Morton Grove, IL: Albert Whitman & Co. Agassi, M. (2000). *Hands Are Not for Hitting*. Minneapolis, MN: Free Spirit Publishing. Hammerseng, K (1996). *Telling Isn't Tattling*. Seattle: Parenting Press.

D. Discuss what children should do if they experience inappropriate touches.

E. Next, children will remove hands from the child figure that are placed in an inappropriate location on the child's body. You may opt to do the activity by asking the children to place the hands either in places that would be considered inappropriate or appropriate.

F. Be sure to review previously taught lesson concepts and connect this to this learning activity. Use visual and other materials to help them build understanding of what is meant by appropriate and inappropriate.

G. Use this activity individually when necessary to address possible concerns.

H. Conclude by reviewing the lesson objectives and by discussing why it is so important to understand the difference between appropriate and inappropriate touches.

Evaluation:

1. Are the children able to distinguish the difference between appropriate and inappropriate touches?

ADDITIONAL SUGGESTIONS FOR SAFETY ACTIVITIES WITH CHILDREN

■ Have students make community service announcements to emphasize the need for safety.

- Invite community members, such as nurses, doctors, firefighters, rescue squad members, school nurses, or local Red Cross representatives, to reinforce safety concepts by visiting the class as guest speakers.

- Focus on choking hazards by planning an activity to bring awareness to this possible danger. Use the choking tube to assess which items are dangerous and may cause choking concerns.

- Focus on fire safety-escape plans by having students consider the importance of fire escape plans. Remind them to avoid hiding in the burning building.

- Focus on freedom from fear by removing fear from your environment by noting the impact fear has on safety.

- Incorporate a Transportation Safety Day into your program.

- Plan skits to demonstrate safety procedures and protocol.

- Write letters to bring awareness to safety issues.

- Incorporate a Safety Awareness Day into your program.

For a listing of children's books that can be used to help children understand safety concepts, please see the "Books for Children" section at the end of this book.

CASE SCENARIOS WITH QUESTIONS TO CONSIDER

Safety Case Scenario #1
You are a first-year teacher who works with experienced teachers of many years. Upon working with this group of teachers, you notice/discover that the experienced teachers frequently omit safety procedures and precautions while working with the children. Supervision is neglected in the hallway as well as on the playground when the director is not present.

Questions to Consider

1. What should you, as the new teacher, do?

2. Should you approach the teachers? If so what would you say?

3. How would you approach the director? What would you say?

4. What are your ethical responsibilities?

Safety Case Scenario #2

Computers are incredible tools of advanced learning. Internet access is readily available and used consistently throughout the day by virtually everyone. Children are learning to use them very skill-fully. The vast information can present many safety concerns for children. The increased threat of children meeting predators online increases this concern.

Questions to Consider

1. What steps could you take to make parents fully aware of the danger of children locating inappropriate and unsafe materials while using the Internet?

2. How will you make students aware of these dangers in appropriate and effective ways?

3. Do you feel the need to have time limits on a child's computer time even if it is used to reinforce educational concepts?

Safety Case Scenario #3

The presence of fear can cause one to experience the inability to process and make wise decisions and choices. The safety of children can be negatively impacted by fear. Those working and inter-acting with children must be mindful of this very fact. Fear causes the body to respond in a reactive state, which in turn causes children to be less likely to weigh the consequences of their actions. Ponder the following questions concerning your interactions and impact of potentially fearful situations for children.

Questions to Consider

1. Do the tones you use with children cause or invoke fear in the children?

2. Do you or your actions promote fear?

3. When a child demonstrates fear, what is your response?

4. What change can you make to your current procedures and interactions with children to insure that it is a fear-free environment?

CURRENT TRENDS IN THE AREA OF SAFETY

Bike Safety

Bike safety must be stressed as a crucial component of safety. Be sure to have children wear a helmet when riding a bicycle as a protective measure in the event of an accident. As stated on the National Safe Kids Campaign's Web site, "bicycles are associated with more childhood injuries than any consumer product except automobile." Half of emergency room injuries are traumatic brain injury. Wearing a helmet can reduce the risk of a head injury by as much as 85 percent.

Bike/Helmet, National Safe Kids. Retrieved 28 May 2005. http://www.SafeKids.org.

Bullying

Bullying among children continues to be a major concern for children, parents and teachers. As stated in *Taking the Bully by the Horns,* "77 percent of students are bullied mentally, verbally and physically and 14 percent of the students have severe reactions to the abuse." (Retrieved, May 24, 2005. http://www hometown.aol.com/kthynoll.) Each of us must take an active role in preventing bullying and removing those who bully others. Children must feel comfortable enough to address these issues with their parents, teachers, or trusted community members. Bullying has a profound effect on the health and safety of any child impacted by such an act.

The Colorado Anti-Bullying Project outlines prevention to bullying entitled STAMP Out Bullying:

- Stay away from bullies
- Tell someone
- Avoid bad situations
- Make friends
- Project confidence

Internet

Unsupervised computer time among children, especially teenagers, can lead to obtaining unsafe material or developing inappropriate companionship on the Internet. When adults fail to supervise children using the Internet, they put children at risk and expose them to inappropriate materials, possible physical molestation (pedophiles), harassment, and legal and financial entrapments. Parents and other responsible adults must reduce these possible risks through awareness and involvement. Outline specific rules that govern a child's time and access to the Internet, such a those defined by Lawrence J. Magid in *Child Safety on the Information Highway* (1998, National Center for Missing and Exploited Children):

- Limit a child's access to certain services and sites.

- Keep track of the child's downloads.

- Know the Internet services your child uses.

- Never allow face-to-face meeting with anyone the child meets on the Internet.

- Never give out identifying information.

- Never respond to obscene messages.

http://www.Safekids.com, Retrieved, 24 May 2005.

Other Areas of Importance

- A greater emphasis is placed on passenger safety for young children. Many states are toughening car seat laws to protect children.

- The issue of SIDS remains a concern for parents and child care providers for infants. Through efforts such as the "Back to Sleep" campaign, experts are making sure that children are put to sleep in a safe way. As a part of these efforts, child day care laws have been put in place so that infants are not put down to sleep on their stomach.

- The increased number of children currently in out-of-home care has prompted groups such as the American Academy of Pediatrics and the American Public Health Association to work toward uniform standards for out-of-home care. The National Health and Safety Performance Standards for Child Care have come out of this partnership.

What Can I Do to Support The Safety of Children in My Care?

- Develop a plan for emergencies.

- Watch out for weather.

- Be well informed.

- Be trained in CPR and first aid.

- Scrutinize the environment.

- Maintain strong supervisory skills.

- Check identification of unfamiliar persons picking up children.

- Remember that how a child is feeling will impact his or her performance level.

- Prevent rushing as it can lead to injuries.

- Involve parents and the communities in educating children about safety procedures and potential safety hazards.

- Prevent injuries for all children, including those with special needs, by providing age-appropriate and developmentally appropriate learning environments.

RESOURCES

Resource for Safety Education
Child Care Law Center
221 Pine Street, 3rd Floor
San Francisco, CA 94104
Online: http://www.childcarelaw.org

Children's Safety Network
National Injury and Violence Prevention Resource Center
55 Chapel Street
Newton, MA 02458-1060
Online: http://www.edc.org

Consumer Product Safety Commission (CPSC)
Washington, DC 20207-0001
Online: http://www.cpsc.gov

National Clearinghouse on Child Abuse and Neglect Information
330 C. Street, SW
Washington, DC 20447
Online: http://www.calib.com

National Fire Protection Association (NFPA)
1 Batterymarch Park
P.O. Box 9101
Quincy, MA 02269-9101
Online: http://www.nfpa.org

National Highway and Transportation Safety Administration (NHTSA)
400 7th Street, SW
Washington, DC 20590
Online: http://www.nhtsa.dot.gov

National Program for Playground Safety
School of Health, Physical Education and Leisure Services

WRC 205, University of Northern Iowa
Cedar Falls, IA 50614-0618
Online: http://www.uni.edu

National Safety Council
1121 Spring Lake Drive
Itasca, IL 60143-3201
Online: http://www.nsc.org

Safe Kids Campaign
1301 Pennsylvania Avenue, NW, Suite
1000 Washington, DC 20004
Online: http://www.safekids.org

State and Territorial Injury Prevention Directors Association
2141 Kingston Court, Suite 110-B
Marletta, GA 30067
Online: http://www.stipda.org

WEB HIGHLIGHTS

The Global Healthy Childcare site was referenced in the previous section but is worth mentioning again because of the user-friendly printable charts that relate to health and safety. Again, this Web site provides a lot of good information relating to guidelines for health and safety that should be observed in the classroom.

http://globalhealthychildcare.org

The Safe Kids Worldwide site is a global network of organizations whose mission is to prevent accidental childhood injury. This Web site provides safety tips to prevent the injuries of children. Brochures, checklists, and videos are also available to use as educational tools.

http://www.safekids.org

The National Program for Playground Safety site contains safety tips and answers important questions about playground safety. Resources and statistics by manufacturer and equipment type are available. A Report Card by State also has useful material. This site also provides detailed information on surfacing materials.

http://www.uni.edu

ASSESSMENT AND OBSERVATION TOOLS FOR NUTRITION

IMPORTANT CONSIDERATIONS FOR PROGRAMS WITH EMPHASIS ON GOOD NUTRITION

Many important things must be considered when planning for good nutrition in the early childhood education environment:

- Realize that safe handling of food and utensils is important.

- Offer a variety of nutritious foods each day.

- Provide nutrition education for children and families.

- Include families in the meal-planning process.

- Model healthy eating practices for children.

- Understand that developmental issues and special needs must be considered when feeding and preparing meals for young children.

- Be informed about food allergies of children in your care.

- Be respectful of cultural differences surrounding eating and food selection.

- Use cooking activities with children as a way to expand their food choices.

DEVELOPMENTAL FACTORS IN EATING BEHAVIORS

With young children, developmental factors must be considered when trying to understand their eating behaviors and plan for them accordingly. Table 12 explains some age-appropriate eating patterns.

TABLE 12   Expected Eating Behaviors According to Age

12–24 months old	has a decreased appetite
	sometimes described as a finicky or fussy eater; may go on food jags
	uses spoon with some degree of skill
	helps feed self
2 years old	appetite is fair
	often has strong likes and dislikes; may go on food jags
	likes simple food, dislikes mixtures, wants food served in familiar ways
	learns table manners by imitating adults and older children
3 years old	appetite is fairly good; prefers small servings, likes only a few cooked vegetables
	feeds self independently, if hungry
	uses spoon in semi-adult fashion; may even spear with fork
	dawdles over food when not hungry
4 years old	appetite fluctuates from very good to fair
	may develop dislikes of certain foods and refuse them to the point of tears if pushed
	likes to help with meal preparation
	uses all eating utensils; becomes skilled at spreading jelly or peanut butter or
	cuts soft foods such as bread
5 years old	eats well, but not at every meal
	likes familiar foods
	often adopts food dislikes of family members and teachers
	makes breakfast (pours cereal, gets out milk and juice) and lunch (spreads peanut butter and jam on bread)

Reprinted with permission, *Health, Safety, and Nutrition for the Young Child,* Marotz, Cross, and Rush, 2005. Thomson Delmar Learning.

It is important to remember that young children need to eat more frequently than adults. Young children usually eat breakfast, morning snack, lunch, afternoon snack, dinner, and bedtime snack.

FOOD GUIDE PYRAMID

MyPyramid.gov
STEPS TO A HEALTHIER YOU

The MyPyramid food guidance system was developed and issued by the United States Department of Agriculture and the Department of Health and Human Services. It emphasizes the principles of the *2005 Guidelines for Americans* and other nutritional standards to assist consumers in making healthier food and physical activity choices. Available at http://www.mypyramid.gov, MyPyramid is an easy-to-use and customizable tool that reflects the most current science.

The key to good nutrition is to eat moderate amounts of a variety of foods. Foods such as fats and sugars should be limited in the diet. A common problem in our society is the portion sizes consumed by individuals. The American Heart Association recommends the following guidelines for good nutrition:

- Eat 6 ounces of lean meat per day. (3 ounces of meat is about the size of a deck of cards.)

- Eat no more than four eggs per week.

- Eat five or more servings of fruits and vegetables per day. (Servings size is a half-cup or one medium piece of fruit.)

- Consume two to four servings of dairy products per day. (Serving size is 1 cup of milk.)

- Eat six servings of breads, cereals, and pasta per day. (Serving size for a child is a half-cup.)

THE FUNCTIONS OF NUTRIENTS

The nutrients necessary for bodily functions can be divided into six categories: carbohydrates, fats, proteins, minerals, vitamins, and water. Each of the nutrients is important to developing and maintaining healthy bodies. Table 13 provides an overview of some functions of nutrients in the body.

TABLE 13   Nutrient Contributions

Nutrient	Important Function for the Body
Carbohydrates (Primarily obtained through breads, cereals, rice, fruits)	Provide energy
Fats (Primarily obtained through oils)	Provide energy
Proteins (Primarily obtained through meat sources, dry beans, eggs, and nuts)	Provide energy, Provide for growth, Provide for regulation
Minerals	Provide for growth, Provide for regulation
Water	Provide for growth, Provide for regulation
Vitamins	Provide for regulation

This information is often simplified in the following manner so that children can easily remember the purpose of different nutrients in the body. Nutrients can be said to help us do three basic things: GO, GROW, and GLOW.

GO = energy

GROW = growth of tissues

GLOW = regulation of bodily processes

RECOMMENDED DIETARY INTAKE

The Food and Nutrition Board gives recommended daily allowances for the nutrients needed for healthy growth and development. The allowances are based on the age and current medical situation of the individual; for example, the recommended intake of certain nutrients might be higher for pregnant and nursing mothers. The following section gives the daily allowances of essential nutrients according to age. For further information on the suggested daily allowances, refer to the Web site of the Food and Drug Administration. (http://www.fda.gov/)

FOOD SOURCES FOR NUTRIENTS

Children can get necessary nutrients from a variety of foods. Children should consume foods that supply carbohydrates, fats, proteins, minerals, vitamins, and water in adequate amounts daily. The MyPyramid can be helpful in making choices for children.

Teachers of young children must understand that the smaller stomach capacity of children requires that they eat the right types of foods to get the proper nutrients for healthy growth and development. The key to a healthy diet is to provide a wide variety of foods high in nutritious value.

Making sure children and adults get the proper amounts of fruits and vegetables in their diet is especially difficult. This is part of the reason for the use of the "5 a Day for Better Health" slogan. Remembering the following points can be helpful:

- Eat five servings of fruits and vegetables daily.

- Eat at least one food rich in Vitamin C each day.

- Eat at least one food rich in Vitamin A each day

- Eat at least one food that is high in fiber each day.

- Eat foods from the cabbage family several times each week (cabbage, broccoli, cauliflower, Brussels sprouts, and so on). (Marotz, 2005)

The following suggestions can be helpful in meeting the "5 a Day" guidelines.

Good to Excellent Sources of Vitamin C

Oranges	Tomatoes
Strawberries	Grapefruit
Cauliflower	Greens, such as spinach and mustard greens
Broccoli	Cabbage
Sweet peppers	Tangerines

Good to Excellent Sources of Vitamin A

Cantaloupe	Pumpkin
Carrots	Sweet potatoes
Spinach	Apricots
Broccoli	Winter squash
Watermelon	

Dietary Fiber Content of Some Commonly Eaten Foods

Cereals	Bananas
Oatmeal	Raisins
Macaroni	Baked potato with skin
Whole wheat bread	Pinto beans
Crackers	Greens beans
Apples with skin	

VITAMIN SUMMARY

Although vitamins are not needed in large amounts, they are crucial to the maintenance of normal bodily functions. Vitamins often act together with other vitamins to perform different functions in the body. If the balance of vitamins in the body is out of proportion, there can be adverse effects. Vitamin levels that are too high can cause toxic symptoms in the body. Vitamins levels that are too low can cause deficiency symptoms. Vitamins that are fat-soluble, such as vitamins A, D, E, and K, remain in the body longer and can be toxic if taken in mega doses (10 times the normal daily allowance). This does not usually happen through food consumption alone. Water-soluble vitamins, such as vitamin C, thiamin, riboflavin, niacin, pantothenic acid, vitamins B6 and B12, folacin, and biotin, are easily passed through the body and do not easily build up toxic effects.

MINERAL SUMMARY

Many bodily functions require that certain minerals be present. Minerals serve many purposes in the body. Minerals, such as calcium, are important for growth of bones and teeth and are also important for regulating muscle contraction and release of insulin. Minerals such as iron are essential to hemoglobin and to the oxygen use of the body. Iron and calcium are only two of the many minerals the body needs.

Minerals are important to bodily functions, but they are needed in appropriate amounts. Once again, the key to good nutrition is to eat a wide variety of healthy foods high in nutrient content.

Sources of Iron

Meats, such as liver, beef, ham, chicken   Grain products

Dried peas, beans, and lentils   Spinach

Prunes and raisins

Sources of Calcium

Milk   Salmon

Cheese   Broccoli

Yogurt

MEAL PATTERNS FOR INFANTS

Feeding and preparing meals for infants is unique in that some babies might be given formula and some might be given breast milk. The development of the infant and the weight of the infant at birth are also factors nutritionally. While infants are small, their caloric needs are relatively high, so they must eat more often to meet that need. The Child and Adult Care Food Program provides guidelines for helping teachers understand typical meal patterns for infants; however, it is important to remember that every infant is unique and may have different needs. The child's doctor will guide this process.

Suggested Child Care Infant Meal Pattern of the Child and Adult Care Food Program

Infants 0–3 months:

- Breakfast
  - 4–6 ounces of formula or breast milk

- Lunch (and the same for dinner)
  - 4–6 ounces of formula or breast milk

- Midday snacks (morning and afternoon)
  - 4–6 ounces of formula or breast milk

Infants 4–7 months:

- Breakfast
  - 4–6 ounces of formula or breast milk
  - 1–3 tablespoons of infant cereal

- Lunch (and the same for dinner)
  - 4–8 ounces of formula or breast milk

- 1–3 tablespoons of infant cereal
- 1–3 tablespoons fruit and/or cereal

- Midday snacks (morning and afternoon)
  - 4–6 ounces of formula or breast milk

Infants 8–11 months:

- Breakfast
  - 6–8 ounces of formula or breast milk
  - 2–4 tablespoons infant cereal
  - 1–4 tablespoons fruit and/or vegetable

- Lunch (and the same for dinner)
  - 6–8 fluid ounces of formula or breast milk
  - 2–4 tablespoons infant cereal
  - 1–4 tablespoons meat or dry beans or ½–2 ounces of cheese or 1–4 tablespoons fruit or vegetable

- Midday snacks (morning and afternoon)
  - 2–4 ounces formula or breast milk
  - ½ slice bread or 1–2 crackers

Refer to Table 14 for a sample chart that can be used as a planning guide.

Meal Patterns for Children Ages 1–12

In the same manner in which developmental issues are always considerations in curriculum planning for children, developmental issues must be considered during meal planning. Certain eating behaviors are typical of preschool children at different ages.

Table 14   Nutrient Contributions

Name and Age of Infant	Breakfast	AM Snack	Lunch	PM Snack

Typical behaviors might include some of the characteristics in Table 15.

Table 15

Age	Eating Behavior
12–24 months	often becomes a picky eater with certain favorites called "food jags"
	appetite may decrease
	begins to learn to use a spoon
	enjoys trying to feed self
2 years old	has strong food preferences
	likes finger foods
	does not like food that is mixed together
3 years old	can feed self independently
	begins to learn to use fork
	appetite is good
	likes small serving sizes
4 years old	develops strong oppositional behaviors to foods that are disliked
	appetite levels fluctuate
	enjoys helping to prepare food and set the table
5 years old	enjoys familiar foods
	often models food preferences after adults
	eats well

Adapted from Marotz 2005.

When planning meals for young children, offering a variety of healthy foods in the correct amounts is essential. The Child and Adult Care Food Program gives guidelines regarding the amounts of food and the types of food that should be included for children of various ages.

Serving Sizes for Young Children
Ages 1–2

Milk/Juice = ½ cup

Vegetable or Fruit = ¼ cup

Meat or Meat Alternative = ½ ounce for snack and 1 ounce for lunch and dinner

Bread = ½ slice

Ages 3–5

Milk/Juice = ¾ cup

Vegetable or Fruit = ½ cup

Meat or Meat Alternative = ½ ounce for snack and 1½ ounce for lunch and dinner

Bread = ½ slice

Ages 6–12

Milk/Juice = 1 cup

Vegetable or Fruit = ¾ cup

Meat or Meat Alternative = 1 ounce for snack and 2 ounces for lunch and dinner

Bread = 1 slice

The following sample menu planner can be helpful as you select foods for meals. Another good reference is *Caring for Our Children*, published by the U.S. Department of Agriculture.

Menu Planning

When planning meals for young children, nutritional value should be completed by the appeal of the food. Combining different colors and textures of food makes the meal more interesting to children. The following chart can be used to easily comply with the suggested meal patterns for children.

Menu Form

BREAKFAST	MONDAY	TUESDAY	WEDNESDAY	THURSDAY	FRIDAY
• Milk					
• Bread					
• Fruit or Vegetable					
MORNING SNACK					
• Bread					
• Fruit/Vegetable					
or					
• Milk					

BREAKFAST	MONDAY	TUESDAY	WEDNESDAY	THURSDAY	FRIDAY

LUNCH
- Protein
- Fruit/Vegetable
- Fruit/Vegetable
- Bread
- Milk

AFTERNOON SNACK
- Bread
- Fruit/Vegetable

or

- Milk

FOOD SAFETY

Programs for young children must always be attentive to sanitation guidelines. This is especially true with food because so many illnesses can be a result of improper handling of food and food utensils or surfaces. Refer to the following sanitation evaluation list for pointers on handling food properly. In addition, check the sanitation guidelines for the state in which the program operates; each state has its own additional requirements.

Basic Suggestions for Sanitation Evaluations
Food

- Supplies of all food must meet all federal and state codes and must have been properly inspected.

- All milk products must be pasteurized.

Food Storage

- Perishable foods must be kept at appropriate temperatures.
  - Refrigerator (40°F)
  - Freezer (0°F)

- Frozen foods must be quick thawed or thawed in the refrigerator.

- Foods must be stored in sealed containers of metal, hard plastic, or glass.

- No food containers should be stored on the floor.

- Food items and nonfood items should be stored separately.

- Storerooms for food should be kept between 50 and 70°F.

Food Preparation and Handling

- Wash all raw fruits and vegetables thoroughly.

- Check the internal temperatures of meat when cooking.

- Maintain potentially hazardous foods at temperatures either below 40° For above 140°F.

- Cover foods during transportation.

- Each serving bowl should have a serving spoon.

- Leftover food from the serving bowls on the table is not saved unless it is fruit that can be thoroughly washed.

PLANNING FOR NUTRITION EDUCATION OPPORTUNITIES

- Additional Suggestions for Nutrition Activities with Children

- Case Scenarios with Questions to Consider

- Current Trends in the Area of Nutrition

- What Can I Do to Support Good Nutrition with the Children in My Care?

ACTIVITY PLANS

Activity Plan # 1: Nutrition: Stone Soup

Concept: Vegetables are healthy foods that must be eaten daily for good health.

Objectives:

- Children will understand the importance of nutrients provided by vegetables.

- Children will develop fine motor skills as they cut slivers of vegetables with plastic knives.

- Children will improve their ability to follow directions as they use the rebus chart with picture directions.

Materials List: Rock, tomatoes, water, salt, pepper, potatoes, corn, onions, carrots, and other various vegetables for soup; copy of the book *Stone Soup;* pots and utensils for making soup.

Learning Activities:

A. In preparation for reading the book *Stone Soup,* show the children the rock and ask them if they would like to eat soup that was made with a stone. Have them brainstorm about the types of things needed to make soup.

B. Ask the children to listen for the types of things that were added to the stone soup as the book is read. Then read the book to the children.

C. After reading the book, show children the basket of vegetables. Lead the children in a discussion about how vegetables help our bodies to grow strong. Ask them to recall which vegetables were used in the story. Explain to the children that they will be helping to make a vegetable soup much like the one in the story.

D. Prepare an area for small groups of children at a time to help wash and prepare the vegetables to put into the soup that the class will make. The items can be cut into small strips so that the children can cut them into smaller pieces with a plastic knife.

E. To enhance literacy development as well, have the children use a rebus chart showing the items needed and the proper amounts required for the soup.

Recipe for Vegetable Soup:

Stew meat or soup bone (if desired)	corn
2 quarts of water	peas
onions	celery
carrots	okra
potatoes	green pepper

Boil soup bone in water until done. Remove meat from bone. Add all other ingredients. Cook slowly for several hours. If too thick, add water. Add salt and pepper to taste.

Evaluation:

1. Were the children able to identify vegetables as an important source of nutrients for the body?

2. Were the children able to cut the items into smaller pieces for use in the soup?

3. Were the children able to follow the directions on the chart to make the soup with the teacher?

Activity Plan #2 Nutrition: Serve It Up

Concept: A variety of types of healthy foods are needed for healthy growth.

Objectives:

- The children will increase their awareness of the different types of foods that should be eaten daily.

- The children will understand the relationship of the food pyramid to their food intake.

- The children will improve their ability to sort items into categories by matching vegetables, fruits, and so on.

Materials List: Large chart of the MyPyramid, pictures of food items needed for a healthy diet (use food guide pyramid for suggestions), large drawing of a plate.

Learning Activities:

A. Show the children the MyPyramid and explain the categories of foods on the chart. Hold up plastic pieces of food or pictures of foods to help children identify which types of food are vegetables, fruits, meats, and so on.

B. Introduce the children to the concept of "5-A-Day." Explain that it means eating five servings of fruits and vegetables each day. Have the children share about their favorite fruits and vegetables.

C. Have the children work in small groups to match the pictures of food items to the category on the MyPyramid.

D. Have a large plate drawn on a poster board. Ask children to select healthy foods for lunch by following this pattern:

Milk

Meat

Fruit

Vegetable

Bread

Evaluation:

1. Did the children understand the differences in the different types of food?

2. Did the children understand the importance of eating a variety of foods each day?

3. Were the children able to select healthy foods for lunch?

Activity Plan #3: Healthy or Unhealthy Choices

Concept: Children can learn the difference between making healthy food choices and making unhealthy food choices.

Objectives:

- Children will be able to identify the difference between healthy food choices and unhealthy food choices.

- Children will complete a matching activity to demonstrate their understanding of which foods are healthy or unhealthy.

Materials List: Construction paper, drawing materials and supplies, magazines or food picture cards, variety of healthy and unhealthy foods, such as fruits, vegetables, and snacks.

Learning Activities:

I. Read about and discuss with the children the definition of healthy and unhealthy. Build motivation by asking questions such as, "Should we eat healthy or unhealthy foods?" "Share with us why you feel this way." "What could happen if you eat healthy food?" "What could happen if you eat unhealthy food?" Be sure to review previously taught lesson concepts and connect them to this learning activity. Use visual and other materials to help the children build understanding of what is meant by healthy and unhealthy. Suggested books to read:

Berenstain, S., & Berenstain, J. (1995). *The Berenstain Bears and Too Much Junk Food.* New York: Random House.

Rockwell, L. (1999). *Good Enough to Eat: A Kid's Guide to Food and Nutrition.* New York: Harper Collins.

J. Plan activities throughout the curriculum to reinforce the lesson concept. For example, make veggie games that allow the children to identify vegetables among many kinds of foods. Plan a parent event centered on eating healthy. The parents will bring in items to make a vegetable soup. Afterward, the children will graph their favorite vegetable. The class could also repeat the activity using fruit.

K. Conclude by reviewing the lesson objectives and by discussing why making healthy versus unhealthy food choices is better for the body.

Evaluation:

1. Are the children able to identify the difference between healthy food choices and unhealthy food choices?

2. Did the children complete a matching activity to demonstrate their understanding of which foods are healthy or unhealthy?

Activity Plan # 4: Water Works Wonders

Concept: Children can learn the importance of water to help the body grow.

Objectives:

- Children will be able to identify the importance of water in their diet as essential to growth and development.

- Children will illustrate two ways to promote drinking enough water each day.

Materials List: Poster board to make graph, variety of flavored and unflavored bottled waters, paper or plastic cups, writing materials, and post-it notes.

Learning Activities:

A. Read and discuss with the children the important role of water in their diet to assist growth and development.

B. Build motivation by asking questions such as, "Why is drinking water so important to our bodies?" "How do you feel when you are thirsty?" Be sure to review previously taught lesson concepts and connect them to this learning activity. Use visual and other materials to help children build an understanding of why drinking water is so important to our bodies.

C. Plan lesson and learning experiences that will build understanding of the importance of water.

D. Have the children participate in a learning experience that centers around the theme of water.

E. Chart, display, and demonstrate results of previously taught concepts and lessons. Follow up each activity with discussion of the importance of water.

F. Conclude by reviewing the lesson objectives.

Evaluation:

1. Can children identify why water in their diet is essential to growth and development?

2. Can children illustrate two ways to promote drinking enough water each day?

ADDITIONAL SUGGESTIONS FOR NUTRITION ACTIVITIES WITH CHILDREN

■ Community Soup Day: Ask the parents to bring in fresh, frozen, or canned vegetables to make a vegetable soup. This is an excellent conclusion activity after learning about the importance of eating vegetables.

■ Allow the children to make a menu book of healthy foods.

■ Visit a grocery store and discuss healthy food selections.

■ Make fruit smoothies, or any of the healthy snacks listed in the Healthy Snacks and Recipes section that follows, and discuss the nutritional value.

■ As you have lunch with the children, discuss the nutritional value of the food served and how this helps the body to grow.

■ Invite a guest speaker (such as a nurse, fitness trainer, chef, or nutritionist) to come to class and share information concerning healthy eating habits, ways to shop for healthy foods, and ways to cook healthier.

■ Use cooking activities as a way to teach cognitive skills as well as nutrition by

  ■ following directions in a recipe.

  ■ classifying foods or utensils into categories.

- making comparisons of how foods are alike and different.

- examining how cooking and freezing changes the textures of foods.

- sequencing the steps used to make a favorite food.

- discussing cause and effect (What makes things happen as they do? What caused the bread to rise?).

- making prediction about what will happen when....

For a listing of children's books that can be used to help children understand nutrition concepts, please see the "Books for Children" section at the end of this book.

Easy Popcorn Balls

1 large bag of marshmallows

6–8 cups of popped corn

1 stick of butter

Melt the marshmallows and butter. Pour over the popped corn. Have the children grease their hands with butter and form the popcorn into balls.

Apple Muffins

½ cup shortening

1 cup sugar

1 teaspoon cinnamon

¾ cup milk

2 cups plain flour

2 teaspoons baking powder

½ teaspoon salt

2 cups chopped apples

Mix the flour, baking powder, and salt together. Cut in shortening. Add other items. Stir and bake in muffin tins for 15 minutes at 350 degrees. If milk is increased, then they can be fried as pancakes on a griddle.

Applesauce

8 apples

⅔ cup sugar

1 cup water

Peel apples. Cut apples into quarters. Throw away the core. Put apples, sugar, and water into a sauce pan. Cook over medium heat until apples are soft. Stir well, cool, and serve.

Butter

½ pint whipping cream

dash salt

Put the whipping cream into a clean plastic shaking jar. Secure lid. Have children take turns shaking the jar until the liquid turns into butter. Spread on crackers or bread to eat.

Party Mix

2 cups of rice chex

2 cups of wheat chex

2 cups of cheerios

2 cups of pretzel sticks

½ cup melted butter

1 pkg. dry ranch style salad dressing mix

Mix all ingredients and place in baking pan. Cook on low heat for 30 minutes. Stir once or twice.

Gelatin Toast

1 pkg. gelatin (any flavor) in a large shaker

soft butter or margarine

sliced bread

Have children spread butter on bread with plastic knives. Shake on powdered gelatin. Toast in oven until butter melts.

Baby Pizzas

2 cans of flaky canned biscuits

1 jar of pizza sauce

1 pkg. grated mozzarella cheese

Have each child pat and form biscuit into individual pizza. Place 1 tablespoon sauce on each pizza. Sprinkle with cheese. Bake 6-8 minutes at 450 degrees on a greased cookie sheet.

Bugs on a Log

washed celery cut into 2 inch strips

peanut butter

raisins

Spread peanut butter on top of celery. Put raisins on top. (Celery can be stuffed with other items such as pimento cheese or cream cheese mixed with pineapple.)

Biscuit Animals

Give each child two canned biscuits. Allow them to use the first one to shape the body and use the other one to form the head and other body parts. Brush the finished animal with melted butter. Sprinkle a mixture of sugar and cinnamon on the animal. Bake according to the directions on the package of canned biscuits.

Sherbet

1 can condensed milk

6 cans orange crush soda

1 pound can crushed pineapple

Place all ingredients into ice cream freezer. Stir to mix well. Freeze according to directions with ice cream freezer.

Ice Cream

1 quart whole milk

1½ teaspoon vanilla

1 can condensed milk

1 pkg. gelatin (any flavor)

Place all ingredients into ice cream freezer. Mix well. Freeze according to directions on ice cream freezer.

Additional Ideas for Nutritious Snacks

- Make fruit kabobs.

- Freeze applesauce or pudding in cups with a popsicle stick.

- Use plain yogurt and have children add fruit and different toppings.

- Freeze peeled bananas on a stick. Remember to coat the bananas in orange juice to prevent discoloration. For fun try adding a little powered gelatin before freezing.

- Combine fruit juice with seltzer water for a healthy drink.

- Don't forget the blender. Many good snacks can be made by putting fruits, ice, and milk into a blender.

CASE SCENARIOS WITH QUESTIONS TO CONSIDER

Nutrition Case Scenario #1

It is often stated that children model what they see adults do. This is equally true concerning what they see adults eat. With increased awareness of the growing concern of obesity in children, how can you as teacher motivate parents and others within the community to model better eating choices in front of children?

Questions to Consider

1. How will you actively motivate parents to model selecting meaningful meal choices in front of children?

2. What will be your primary way of recruiting others to help you inform the community of this pressing need?

3. How will you involve children in this awareness campaign without creating tension among them and their parents?

Nutrition Case Scenario #2

You have a four-year-old child in your class who weights 145 pounds. She refuses to eat any vegetables. The only foods the child will eat consist of high levels of sugar and fat. You notice that she does not have enough energy to play outside and is often found sleeping in class. The father of the child says the child will not eat anything but junk food and hamburgers. The other children in the class are beginning to refuse to eat their food and state that the Sue doesn't eat unless she gets what she wants.

Questions to Consider

1. What is your role in such a situation?

2. What is the parent's role in such a situation?

3. How would you address this concern with the parent?

4. How would you address this concern with the children?

5. What are the current and long-term concerns for Sue?

Nutrition Case Scenario #3

The pursuit to eat healthy is often blocked by the cost of eating highly nutritious foods. As you seek to motivate others to make beneficial choices concerning their food selections and consumption, how will you address the growing concern of the cost to eat nutritiously?

Questions to Consider

1. What can you do to encourage parents and others to continue to eat healthy despite the cost of eating this way?

2. Who can you contact to assist or address this concern on the local, state, and national level?

3. Share what you would include in a plan to share with parents on how they could eat well in a reasonably inexpensive way.

CURRENT TRENDS IN THE AREA OF NUTRITION

Obesity

Childhood obesity has become a major problem among America's children for several reasons:

■ Decreased lack of exercise and a general sedentary life style.

- Increased consumption of foods high in fats and sugars.

- The hurried pace and stress of many families' life styles leave little time for family fitness and an insufficient amount of mental strength needed to resist the temptation to eat the wrong types of foods.

Children in the United States have higher cholesterol levels than children in any other county, which is also a result of consuming fatty food and getting little or no exercise. There is an increased concern over the amount of preservatives and additives that are used in foods today.

Obesity in children can lead to many troubling healthy concerns, including juvenile diabetes. To counteract these troubling concerns, children should be encouraged to make healthy food choices, exercise, and get plenty of rest.

Many child and youth fitness programs have been put into place in an effort to increase the physical fitness and nutrition of America's youth. The 5-A-Day campaign has begun as an effort to encourage children and adults to eat five servings of fruits and vegetables each day as part of a healthy diet.

The hurried life styles of families often make eating meals together a forgotten pleasure. This makes it even more important for teachers and children to sit down together at mealtimes where they can enjoy a relaxed meal with pleasant conversation. It is important to have enough teachers so that each teacher can sit with a small group of children.

Teachers should always be aware that as our nation and classroom become more diverse in population, food and eating practices are not the same in every culture. Therefore, teachers should use this diversity as an opportunity to learn more about food preferences and the cultural issues surrounding eating.

Stress

Stress continues to be on the rise. Combating stress places emphasis on prevention and removal of what causes the stress. Focusing on health, safety, and nutrition choices can help eliminate stress.

WHAT CAN I DO TO SUPPORT GOOD NUTRITION WITH THE CHILDREN IN MY CARE?

- Educate children and families about good nutrition.

- Become an avenue of learning for children and parents.

- Make selecting good nutrition choices a part of your learning opportunities.

- Be a role model of good nutrition choices.

- Spend mealtime with your students and discuss the importance of eating healthfully.

- Build learning experiences around healthy food choices and practices that will promote good nutrition.

- Be careful to understand and follow the nutritional guidelines and regulations.

- Maintain accurate and up-to-date health records on the children to avoid food allergy concerns.

- Involve the community and especially parents in helping to promote good nutrition.

- Use the Mindful of Maximizing a Child's Potential Questionnaire and the Tracking Your Success form earlier in this book to encourage parents to be active participants in this important awareness campaign to promote good nutrition.

RESOURCES

Resources for Nutrition

American Diabetes Association
1701 North Beauregard Street
Alexandria, VA 22311
Online: http://www.diabetes.org

American Dietetic Association
216 West Jackson Boulevard
Chicago, IL 60606-6995
Online: http://www.eatright.org

Food and Nutrition Information Center
Agricultural Research Service, USDA
10301 Baltimore Avenue
Beltsville, MD 20705
Online: http://www.nal.usda.gov

Food Research Action Center
1875 Connecticut Avenue, NW Suite 540
Washington, DC 20009
Online: http://www.frac.org

National Association of WIC Directors
2001 S Street, NW Suite 580
Washington, DC 20009
Online: http://www.nwica.org

Society for Nutrition Education
9202 N. Meridian Street, Suite 200
Indianapolis, IN 46260
Online: http://www.sne.org

U.S. Food and Drug Administration
5600 Fishers Lane
Rockville, MD 20857-0001
Online: http://www.fda.gov

USDA Food and Nutrition Service
3101 Park Center Drive
Alexandria, VA 22302
Online: http://www.fns.usda.gov

USDA Food Safety and Inspection Service
U. S. Department of Agriculture
Washington, DC 20250-3700
Online: http://www.fsis.usda.gov

WEB HIGHLIGHTS

The 5-A-Day for Better Health Web site has great information on
how to incorporate fruits and vegetables into the daily diet.

http://www.5aday.com

The Healthy People 2010 Web site has interesting ideas and information on the national efforts to eat better and be fit. It contains a wealth of information and is certainly an example of how health, safety, and nutrition are intricately intertwined.

http://www.healthypeople.gov

BOOKS FOR CHILDREN

Reading aloud is a wonderful gift you can give to children. Through sharing an interesting book, you introduce children to a world they might not otherwise be able to visit. Through books, you can travel anywhere you like, have experiences outside the realm of your current environment, participate in wonderful fantasies, and be saddened and then uplifted.

Children's desire to read and the ability to do so is fostered by reading to them as soon as they are born. Even babies can enjoy looking at picture books and hearing simple stories. Preschoolers love to have favorite books read to them repeatedly. As children move into the school years, they can sustain their interest in longer books that are divided into chapters. When they realize the joy that comes from good books, they are more motivated to read on their own.

Many textbooks provide suggestions for setting up reading corners and providing books for children to read by themselves. This section focuses on books that you can read aloud to children in small or large groups. Remember that the more you read, the better you will become at doing so. When the books have been enjoyed in a group setting, add them to the book corner for children to read alone. In addition, teachers often create lending arrangements where children can take home books for their parents to read and then return. Teachers who believe in the importance of reading choose the best of children's literature and involve families in reading.

The following is an extensive list of children's books, broken down by topic area, which can be used in your health, safety, and nutrition curriculum.

DENTAL HEALTH

Civardi, A. (1992). *Going to the Dentist.* Usborne, London: E. D. C. Publications.

Dowdy, L. (1997). *Barney Goes to the Dentist.* New York: Lyrick.

Frost, H. (1999). *Going to the Dentist.* Mankato, MN: Pebble Books.

Keller, L. (2000). *Open Wide: Tooth School Inside.* New York: Henry Holt & Company.

Lewison, W. (2002). *Clifford's Loose Tooth.* New York: Scholastic.

Mayer, M. (2001). *Just Going to the Dentist.* New York: Golden Books.

McGuire, L. (1993). *Brush Your Teeth Please.* New York: Reader's Digest.

Minarik, E. (2002). *Little Bear's Loose Tooth.* New York: HarperFestival.

Munsch, R. (2002). *Andrew's Loose Tooth.* New York: Scholastic.

Murkoff, H. (2002). *What to Expect When You Go to the Dentist.* New York: HarperFestival.

Rogers, R. (1989). *Going to the Dentist.* New York: G. P. Putman & Sons.

Schoberle, C. (2000). *Open Wide! A Visit to the Dentist.* New York: Simon Spotlight.

Showers, P. (1991). *How Many Teeth?* New York: HarperCollins.

Smee, N. (2000). *Freddie Visits the Dentist.* Hauppauge, NY: Barrons Educational Series.

ILLNESS/GERMS

Berger, M. (1995). *Germs Make Me Sick!* New York: HarperCollins.

Berger, M. (2002). *Why I Sneeze, Shiver, Hiccup, & Yawn.* New York: HarperCollins.

Capeci, A. (2001). *The Giant Germ.* New York: Scholastic Paperbacks.

Cole, J. (1995). *The Magic School Bus Inside Ralphie: A Book About Germs.* New York: Scholastic.

Cote, P. (2002). *How Do I Feel?* New York: Houghton Mifflin. (Spanish & English).

Dealey, E. (2002). *Goldie Locks Has Chicken Pox.* New York: Scholastic.

Demuth, P. (1997). *Achoo!: All About Colds.* New York: Grosset & Dunlap.

Katz, B. (1996). *Germs! Germs! Germs!* New York: Cartwheel Books.

O'Brien-Palmer, M. (1999). *Healthy Me: Fun Ways to Develop Good Health and Safety Habits: Activities for Children 5–8.* Chicago, IL: Chicago Review Press.

Rice, J. (1997). *Those Mean, Nasty, Dirty, Downright Disgusting but Invisible Germs.* St. Paul, MN: Redleaf Press.

Romanek, T. (2003). *Achoo: The Most Interesting Book You'll Ever Read About Germs.* Toronto: Kids Can Press.

Ross, T. (2000). *Wash Your Hands!* New York: Kane/Miller.

Showers, P. (1991). *Your Skin and Mine.* New York: HarperCollins.

Wenkman, L. (1999). *Body Buddies Say . . . "Wash Your Hands!"* Bloomington, IN: Sunrise Publications.

MENTAL HEALTH (FEELINGS)

Agassi, M. (2000). *Hands Are Not for Hitting.* Minneapolis, MN: Free Spirit Publishing.

Anglund, J. (1993). *A Friend Is Someone Who Likes You.* New York: Harcourt Brace Jovanovich.

Anholt, C. (1998). *What I Like.* Cambridge, MA: Candlewick Press.

Anholt, C. (1998). *What Makes Me Happy?* Cambridge, MA: Candlewick Press.

Baker, L. (2001). *I Love You Because You're You.* New York: Cartwheel Books.

Bang, M. (1999). *When Sophie Gets Angry—Really, Really Angry.* New York: Scholastic.

Blumenthal, D. (1999). *The Chocolate-Covered-Cookie Tantrum.* New York: Clarion Books.

Cain, J. (2000). *The Way I Feel.* Seattle, WA: Parenting Press.

Carle, E. (2000). *The Grouchy Ladybug.* New York: Scholastic.

Carle, E. (1999). *The Very Lonely Firefly.* New York: Philomel Books.

Carlson, N. (1997). *How to Lose All Your Friends.* New York: Puffin Books.

Carlson, N. (1990). *I Like Me!* Parsippany, NJ: Pearson Learning.

Cole, J. (1997). *I'm a Big Brother.* New York: William Morrow & Co.

Cole, J. (1997). *I'm a Big Sister.* New York: William Morrow & Co.

Crary, E. (1992). *I'm Mad.* Seattle, WA: Parenting Press.

Crary, E. (1996). *I'm Scared.* Seattle, WA: Parenting Press.

Cruz, R. (1992). *Alexander and the Terrible, Horrible, No Good, Very Bad Day.* New York: Aladdin.

Cutis, J. L. (2002). *I'm Gonna Like Me: Letting Off a Little Self-Esteem.* New York: Joanna Cotler.

Cutis, J. L. (1998). *Today I Feel Silly: And Other Moods That Make My Day.* New York: HarperCollins.

Demi. (1996). *The Empty Pot.* New York: Henry Holt & Co.

Eisnberg, P. (1992). *You're My Nikki.* New York: Dial Books for Children.

Gainer, C. (1998). *I'm Like You, You're Like Me: A Child's Book About Understanding and Celebrating Each Other.* Minneapolis, MN: Free Spirit Publishing.

Hammerseng, K. (1996). *Telling Isn't Tattling.* Seattle, WA: Parenting Press.

Henkes, K. (1996). *Chrysanthemum.* New York: HarperTrophy.

Hudson, C., & Ford, B. (1990). *Bright Eyes, Brown Skin.* Orange, NJ: Just Us Books.

Krasny, L., & Brown, M. (2001). *How to Be a Friend: A Guide to Making Friends and Keeping Them.* Boston: Little Brown & Co.

Kubler, A., & Formby, C. (1995). *Come Play with Us.* Ashworth Road, Bridgemead, Swindon, Wiltshire: Child's Play International, Ltd.

Lachner, D. (1995). *Andrew's Angry Words.* New York: North South Books.

Lalli, J. (1997). *I Like Being Me: Poems for Children, About Feeling Special, Appreciating Others, and Getting Along.* Minneapolis, MN: Free Spirit Publishing.

Lewis, J. (1993). *Claire and Friends.* Brookline, MA: Creative License Press.

Lewis, P. (2002). *I'll Always Love You.* Wilton, CT: Tiger Tales.

Lovell, P. (2001). *Stand Tall, Molly Lou Melon.* New York: Scholastic.

Naylor, P. (1994). *King of the Playground.* New York: Aladdin.

O'Neill, A. (2002). *The Recess Queen.* New York: Scholastic.

Parr, T. (2001). *It's Okay to be Different.* Boston, MA: Little, Brown.

Payne, L. (1994). *Just Because I Am: A Child's Book of Affirmation.* Minneapolis, MN: Free Spirit Publishing.

Payne, L. (1997). *We Can Get Along: A Child's Book of Choices.* Minneapolis, MN: Free Spirit Publishing.

Pinkney, A., & Pinkney, B. (1997). *Pretty Brown Face.* Lake Worth, FL: Red Wagon Books.

Spelman, C. (2000). *When I Feel Angry.* New York: Albert Whitman & Co.

Thomas, P. (2000). *Stop Picking on Me.* Hauppauge, NY: Barrons.

Vail, R. (2002). *Sometimes I'm Bombaloo.* New York: Scholastic.

Viorst, J. (1992). *The Good-bye Book.* New York: Aladdin.

Weninger, B., & Marks, A. (1995). *Good-bye Daddy.* New York: North-South Books.

PERSONAL HEALTH & SELF-CARE

Aliki. (1992). *I'm Growing.* New York: HarperCollins.

Aliki. (1991). *My Five Senses.* New York: HarperCollins.

Brown, M. (1991). *Good Night Moon.* New York: HarperFestival.

Cazet, D. (1992). *I'm Not Sleepy.* New York: Orchard Books.

Edwards, F. (1990). *Mortimer Mooner Stopped Taking a Bath.* Kingston, Ontario: Pokeweed Press.

Fox, M. (1997). *Time for Bed.* Lake Worth, FL: Red Wagon Books.

Gordon, J. R. (1991). *Six Sleepy Sheep.* New York: St. Martin's Press.

Himmelman, J. (1995). *Lights Out!* Mahwah, NJ: Troll.

Katz, A. (2001). *Take Me Out of the Bathtub.* New York: Scholastic.

Keats, E. J. (1992). *Dreams.* New York: Aladdin Books.

Leonard, M. (1998). *Getting Dressed.* New York: Bantam Books.

Murkoff, H. (2000). *What to Expect at Bedtime.* New York: HarperFestival.

Murkoff, H. (2000). *What to Expect When You Go to the Doctor.* New York: HarperFestival.

Pfeffer, W. (1999). *Sounds All Around.* New York: HarperCollins.

Reidy, H. (1999). *What Do You Like to Wear?* New York: Larousse Kingfisher Chambers.

Rowland, P. (1996). *What Should I Wear?* New York: Random House.

Showers , P. (1997). *Sleep Is for Everyone.* New York: HarperCollins.

Showers, P. (1993). *The Listening Walk.* New York: HarperTrophy.

Showers, P. (1990). *Ears Are for Hearing.* New York: Ty Crowell Co.

Sykes, J. (1996). *I Don't Want to Go to Bed.* Wilton, CT: Tiger Tales.

Time-Life. (1993). *What Is a Bellybutton?* Alexandria, VA: Time-Life Books.

Watanabe, S. (1992). *How Do I Put It On?* New York: Philomel.

Wood, A. (1996). *The Napping House.* San Diego, CA: Harcourt Brace & Co.

SAFETY

Berenstain, S., & Berenstain, J. (1999). *My Trusty Car Seat: Buckling Up for Safety.* New York: Random House.

Best, C. (1995). *Red Light, Green Light, Mama and Me.* New York: Orchard Books.

Boxall, E. (2002). *Francis the Scaredy Cat.* Cambridge, MA: Candlewick Press.

Committee, C. B. (2000). *Buckles Buckles Everywhere.* Columbia, SC: Palmetto Bookworks.

Cuyler, M. (2001). *Stop, Drop, Roll.* New York: Simon & Schuster.

Dubowski, C. (1990). *Fire Engine to the Rescue.* New York: McClanahan Book Company.

Girard, L. (1987). *My Body Is Private.* Morton Grove, IL: Albert Whitman & Co.

Hayward, L. (2001). *A Day in the Life of a Firefighter.* New York: Dorling Kindersley Publisher.

Hindman, J. (1986). *A Very Touching Book . . . for Little People and Big People.* Alexandria, VA: Alexandria Press.

Johnsen, K. (1986). *Trouble with Secrets.* Seattle, WA: Parenting Press.

MacLean, C. K. (2002). *Even Firefighters Hug Their Moms.* New York: Dutton.

Mitton, T. (2001). *Down by the Cool of the Pool.* New York: Orchard Books.

Palatini, M. (2002). *Earthquack!* New York: Simon & Schuster.

Prigger, M. (2002). *Aunt Minnie and the Twister.* New York: Clarion.

Rathmann, P. (1995). *Officer Buckle and Gloria.* New York: Putnam.

Reasoner, C. (2003). *Bee Safe (The Bee Attitudes).* Los Angeles, CA: Price Stern Sloan Publishers.

Rylan, C. (1991). *Night in the Country.* New York: Aladdin.

Schwartz, L. (1995). *The Safety Book for Active Kids: Teaching Your Child How to Avoid Everyday Dangers.* Santa Barbara, CA: Learning Works.

Tekavec, H. (2002). *Storm Is Coming!* New York: Dial.

Weeks, S. (2002). *My Somebody Special.* San Diego, CA: Harcourt, Inc.

Weidner, T. (1997). *Your Body Belongs to You.* Morton Grove, IL: Albert Whitman & Co.

SPECIAL NEEDS

Aseltine, L., Mueller, E., & Tait, N. (1987). *I'm Deaf and It's Okay.* Morton Grove, IL: Albert Whitman & Co.

Bunnett, R. (1996). *Friends at School.* Long Island City, NY: Star Bright Books.

Fassler, J. (1987). *Howie Helps Himself.* Morton Grove, IL: Albert Whitman & Co.

Gosselin, K. (1998). *Taking Diabetes to School.* Valley Park, MO: JayJo Books.

Gosselin, K. (1996). *Zooallergy: A Fun Story About Allergy and Asthma Triggers.* Valley Park, MO: JayJo Books

Harrison, T. (1998). *Aaron's Awful Allergies.* Buffalo, NY: Kids Can Press.

Lakin, P. (1994). *Dad and Me in the Morning.* Morton Grove, IL: Albert Whitman & Co.

London , J. (1997). *The Lion Who Had Asthma.* Morton Grove, IL: Albert Whitman & Co.

Maguire, A. (2000). *Special People, Special Ways.* Arlington, TX: Future Horizons.

Mayer, G., & Mayer, M. (1993). *A Very Special Critter.* New York: Golden Books.

Millman, I. (2000). *Moses Goes to School.* New York: Frances Foster Books/Farrar, Straus & Giroux.

Nausau, E. (2001). *The Peanut Butter Jam*. Albuquerque, NM: Health Press. (Allergies)

Powers, M. (1987). *Our Teacher's in a Wheelchair*. Morton Grove, IL: Albert Whitman & Co.

Shriver, M. (2001). *What's Wrong with Timmy?* New York: Little Brown & Co.

Stuve-Bodeen, S. (1998). *We'll Paint the Octopus Red*. Bethesda, MD: Woodbine House.

Weiner, E. (1999). *Taking Food Allergies to School*. Valley Park, MO: JayJo Books.

White Pirner, C. (1994). *Even Little Kids Get Diabetes*. Morton Grove, IL: Albert Whitman & Co.

NUTRITION

Appleton, J. (2001). *Do Carrots Make You See Better?* St. Paul, MN: Red Leaf Press.

Barkan, J. & Wheeler, J. (1989). *My Measuring Cup*. New York: Warner Juvenile Books.

Berenstain, S., & Berenstain, J. (1995). *The Berenstain Bears and Too Much Junk Food*. New York: Random House.

Carle, E. (1998). *Pancakes, Pancakes!* New York: Aladdin Books.

Carle, E. (1986). *The Very Hungry Caterpillar*. New York: Putnam.

Cole, J. (1990). *The Magic School Bus: Inside the Human Body*. New York: Scholastic.

Compestine, Y. (2001). *The Runaway Rice Cake*. New York: Simon & Schuster.

French, V. (1998). *Oliver's Fruit Salad*. New York: Orchard Books.

Geeslin, C. (1999). *How Nanita Learned to Make Flan*. New York: Atheneum.

Gershator, D. (1998). *Bread Is for Eating*. New York: Henry Holt.

Hall, Z. (1996). *The Apple Pie Tree*. New York: Scholastic.

Harms, T. (1981). *Cook and Learn: Nutritious Foods from Various Cultures*. St. Paul, MN: Red Leaf Press.

Katzen, M. (1994). *Pretend Soup and Other Real Recipes: A Cookbook for Preschoolers and Up*. Berkeley, CA: Tricycle Press.

Krauss, R. (1989). *The Carrot Seed*. New York: HarperTrophy.

Lin, G. (2001). *Dim Sum for Everyone*. New York: Knopf.

Lin, G. (1999). *The Ugly Vegetables*. Watertown, MA: Charlesbridge Publishing.

Loreen, L. (1996). *The Edible Pyramid: Good Eating Every Day*. New York: Holiday House.

Mayer, M. (1998). *The Mother Goose Cookbook: Rhymes and Recipes for the Very Young*. New York: William Morrow & Co.

McGinley, N. (1999). *Pigs in the Pantry: Fun with Math and Cooking*. New York: Simon & Schuster.

Paulsen, G. (1998). *The Tortilla Factory*. San Diego, CA: Harcourt Brace.

Peterson, C. (1996). *Harvest Year*. Honesdale, PA: Boyds Mill Press.

Priceman, M. (1996). *How to Make an Apple Pie and See the World*. New York: Knopf.

Reiser, L. (1998). *Tortillas and Lullabies*. New York: Greenwillow Books.

Rockwell, L. (1999). *Good Enough to Eat: A Kid's Guide to Food and Nutrition*. New York: HarperCollins.

Sanger, A. (2001). *First Book of Sushi*. Berkeley, CA: Tricycle Press.

Sharmat, M. (1989). *Gregory, the Terrible Eater*. New York: Scholastic.

Swain, G. (1999). *Eating*. St. Paul, MN: Red Leaf Press.

Wells, P. (2003). *Busy Bears: Breakfast with the Bears*. London, England: Sterling Publications.

Westcott, N. (1998). *Never Take a Pig Out to Lunch and Other Poems*. New York: Orchard Books.

Woods, D., & Woods, A. (2000). *The Big Hungry Bear*. Swindon, England: Child's Play Publishers.

PROFESSIONAL ORGANIZATIONS

When looking to further your development, a professional organization is a great place to start. There are several organizations, some of which even have state or local affiliates.

National Association for the Education of Young Children (NAEYC)
1509 16th Street, NW
Washington, DC 20036
800-424-2460
http://www.naeyc.org
E-mail membership@naeyc.org

Specific membership benefits:
Comprehensive members receive all the benefits of regular membership plus annually receive five or six books immediately after their release by NAEYC.

Regular and student member benefits:

- Six issues of *Young Children,* which includes timely articles on pertinent issues, as well as suggestions and strategies for enhancing children's learning

- Reduced registration fees at NAEYC-sponsored local and national conferences and seminars

- Discounted prices on hundreds of books, videos, brochures, and posters from NAEYC's extensive catalog of materials

Access to the Members Only Web site, including links to additional resources and chat sites for communication with other professionals

National Association of Child Care Professionals (NACCP)
P.O. Box 90723
Austin, TX 78709
800-537-1118
http://www.naccp.org

Specific membership benefits:

Management Tools of the Trade™
Your membership provides complete and FREE access (a $79 value) to these effective management tools that provide technical assistance in human resource management. In addition, you will receive NACCP's quarterly trade journals, *Professional Connections©, Teamwork©,* and *Caring for Your Children©,* to help you stay on top of hot issues in child care. Each edition also includes a Tool of the Trade™.

National Child Care Association (NCCA)
1016 Rosser St.
Conyers, GA 30012
800-543-7161
http://www.nccanet.org

Specific membership benefits:
As the only recognized voice in Washington DC, NCCA has great influence on our legislators. Professional development opportunities are also available.

Association for Education International (ACEI)
The Olney Professional Building
17904 Georgia Avenue, Suite 215
Olney, MD 20832
800-423-2563 or 301-570-2122
301-570-2212 (fax)
http://www.acei.org

ACEI is an international organization dedicated to promoting the best educational practices throughout the world.

Specific membership benefits:

- Workshops and travel/study tours abroad
- Four issues per year of the *Childhood Education* journal and the *Journal of Research in Childhood Education*

■ Hundreds of resources for parents and teachers, including books, pamphlets, audiotapes, and videotapes

National AfterSchool Association (NAA)
1137 Washington Street
Boston, MA 02124
617-298-5012
617-298-5022 (fax)
http://www.naaweb.org

NAA is a national organization dedicated to providing information, technical assistance, and resources concerning children in out-of-school programs. Members include teachers, policy makers, and administrators representing all public, private, and community-based sectors of after-school programs.

Specific member benefits:

■ A subscription to the NAA journal, *School-Age Review*
■ A companion membership in state affiliates
■ Discounts on NAA publications and products
■ Discount on NAA annual conference registration
■ Opportunity to be an NAA accreditation endorser
■ Public policy representatives in Washington, DC

Other Organizations to Contact
The Children's Defense Fund
25 E. St. NW
Washington, DC 20001
202-628-8787
http://www.childrensdefense.org

National Association for Family Child Care
P.O. Box 10373
Des Moines, IA 50306
800-359-3817
http://www.nafcc.org
Journal: *The National Perspective*

National Black Child Development Institute
1023 15th Ave. NW
Washington, DC 20002
202-833-2220
http://www.nbcdi.org

National Head Start Association
1651 Prince Street

Alexandria, VA 22314
703-739-0875
http://www.nhsa.org
Journal: *Children and Families*

International Society for the Prevention of Child Abuse and Neglect
25 W. 560 Geneva Road, Suite L2C
Carol Stream, IL 60188
630-221-1311
http://ispcan.org
Journal: *Child Abuse and Neglect: The International Journal*

Council for Exceptional Children
1110N. Glebe Road, Suite 300,
Arlington, VA 22201
888-CEC-SPED
http://www.cec.sped.org
Journal: *CEC Today*

National Association for Bilingual Education
Union Center Plaza
810 First Street, NE
Washington, DC 20002
http://www.nabe.org
Journal: *NABE Journal of Research and Practice*

International Reading Association
800 Barksdale Road
P.O. Box 8139
Newark, DE 19714
800-336-READ
http://www.reading.org
Journal: *The Reading Teacher*

National Education Organization (NEA)
1201 16th St. NW
Washington, DC 20036
202-833-4000
http://www.nea.org
Journals: *Works4Me* and *NEA Focus,* by online subscription

Zero to Three: National Center for Infants, Toddlers, and Families
2000M. Street NW, Suite 200
Washington, DC 20036
202-638-1144
http://www.zerotothree.org
Journal: *Zero to Three*

REFERENCES

Aronson, S. S., & Spahr, P. M. (2002). *Healthy young children: A manual for programs.* Washington, DC: National Association for the Education of Young Children.

National Safe Kids. Bike/Helmet, National Safe Kids. Retrieved 28 May 2005, from http://www.safekids.org

National Highway and Transportation Safety Administration. Child Passenger Safety. Retrieved 30 May 2005, from http://www.nhtsa .dot.gov/nhtsa/whatis/regions/Region070/07cps.html

Marotz, L. R., Cross, M. Z., & Rush, J. M. (2005). *Health, safety, and nutrition for the young child* (6th ed.). Clifton Park, NY: Thomson Delmar Learning.

Magid, L. J. Child Safety on the Information Highway. Retrieved 24 May 2005, from http://www.safekids.org

Robertson, C. (2003). *Safety, nutrition, and health in early childhood education* (2nd ed.). Clifton Park, NY: Thomson Delmar Learning.

Noll, K. Taking the Bully by the Horns. Retrieved May 24, 2005, from http://www.hometown.aol.com/kthynoll